Regimental History 1914-1920 93rd Burma Infantry

Edited by

John Wilson & Stephen Ede-Borrett

Gosling Press

This edition copyright Gosling Press 2025

All rights reserved

ISBN 978-1-874351-32-0 (Hardback)

ISBN 978-1-874351-33-7 (Paperback)

Gosling Press

www.goslingpress.co.uk

Introduction

Originally raised in 1800 as the 1st Battalion of the 17th Regiment of Madras Native infantry, in 1824 it was redesignated as the 33rd regiment of Madras Native infantry. Originally comprising of Muslims, in 1890 it became a mixed class regiment with Punjabi Muslims, Sikhs and Pathans and was permanently based in Burma where it was used to pacify the rebellions of the hill tribes who lived in the frontier regions of Burma. As part of the 1903 reforms all former Madras units had 60 added to their numbers thus becoming the 93rd Burma Infantry. The battalion returned to India in 1913 being stationed at Barrackpore. In 1914 the class composition of the regiment was 4 companies of Sikhs and 4 of Punjabi Muslims.

On being mobilised for the first world war the regiment was one of 8 infantry battalions dispatched to Egypt to help guard the Suez Canal. In September the regiment moved to France to join the 19th Dehra Dun Brigade in the 7th Meerut Division. The regiment was withdrawn from France in late 1915 and sent to Mesopotamia where it joined the 9th Indian Brigade in the 3rd Lahore Division.

Finally, of note the author of the charming book the Indian Army ABC Myauk was a pseudonym for Captain John William Jerome Alves, originally Commissioned into the King's Own Scottish Borderers as a 2nd Lieutenant on 11 Aug 1900. He was later promoted to Lieutenant on 11 Nov

1902. He transferred to the Indian Army on 13 Feb 1907 and was posted to the 93rd Burma Infantry. Promoted to Captain on 11 Aug 1909 serving as a double company officer. Promoted again to Major on 1 Sep 1915.

Contents

	Introduction	
	Contents	
	Illustrations	
	Abbreviations	
	Part 1 Egypt	
I	Egypt, November 1914 – September 1915	1
	Part II France	
II	France, September, 1915 – December, 1915	12
	Part III MESOPOTAMIA	
III	First Battle of Hannah, 21 January 1916	21
IV	Battle of Duyar Lanh, 8 March, 1916	32
V	Battle of Beit Aeissa, 17 April 1916	45
VI	Battle of The Apex, 24 April 1916	61
VII	Hot Weather, 1916	67
VIII	Operations in The Mahomed Abdul Hassan Bend, December 1916 – January 1917	79
IX	Baghdad	94
X	Battle of The Jebel Hamrin, 25 March 1917	102
XI	The Euphrates Treks	113
XII	Beled and Samarra	126
	Part IV PALESTINE	
XIII	Hot Weather, 1918	133
XIV	The Battle of Brown Hill and After	139
XV	Damascus	148
	Appendix	154

Illustrations

1	The Suez Canal, 1914-1915	7
2	France – The Indian Corps Front 1915	14
3	Skeikh Saad – Kut, January – March 1916. Chapters III and IV	23
4	The Battle of Dujailah. Chapter IV	37
5	Sanna-Beit Aeissa. Chapter V	49
6	The Battles of Beit Aeissa and Apex. Chapters V and VI	63
7	Shumran to Twin Canals. Chapters VII, VIII and IX	71
8	Mahomed Abdul Hassan Bend. Chapter VIII	83
9	Kut to Shahroban. Chapters IX and X	100
10	The Jebel Hamrin. Chapter X	107
11	Samarra, Baghdad, and the Euphrates. Chapters XI and XII	123
12	Palestine and Syria. Chapters XIII, XIV and XV	135
13	Brown Hill to Nablus. Chapters XIII, XIV and XV	145

Abbreviations

A.T.	Army Transport
C.F.A.	Combined Field Ambulance
D.C.	Double-Company
D.S.O.	Distinguished Service Order
E.E.F.	Egyptian Expeditionary Force
E.P. Tents	European Pattern
G.H.Q.	General Headquarters
G.O.C.	General Officer Commanding
H.L.I.	Highland Light Infantry
I.A.R.	Indian Army Reserve
I.D.S.M.	Indian Distinguished Service Medal
I.F.A.	Indian Field Ambulance
I.M.S.	Indian Medical Service
I.O.M.	Indian Order of Merit
M.C.	Military Cross
M.G. Section	Machine Gun section
M.O.	Medical Officer
O.C.	Officer Commanding / Commanding Officer
O.P.	Observation Post
P.M.	Punjabi Muselmen
S and T	Supply and Transport
S.A.A.	Small Arms Ammunition
S.A.S.	Sub Assistant Surgeon

PART I

EGYPT

Chapter I
Egypt, November 1914 – September 1915

When the war broke out in August, 1914, the 93rd Burma Infantry was stationed at Barrackpore, under orders to Jhelum. As the regiment at Barrackpore is liable to be called on for the interior defence of Calcutta, and as instructions had already been received to send a draft of one British officer, two Indian officers, and 93 men to our linked battalion, the 92nd Punjabis, who were mobilising, no one entertained any great hopes of the regiment going on service. It was, moreover, popularly supposed that the war would be over in a few months' time, so that the chances of our hopes being realised appeared to decrease as the days passed.

At this time 2nd Lieutenant S. S. Hodson joined the battalion from the Indian Army Reserve of Officers, a force practically unknown to regulars before the war.

In due course the draft for the 92nd Punjabis left, under the command of Major Simpson, and preparations went on rapidly for the move to Jhelum.

On 15 October, to the delight and astonishment of everyone, orders came to mobilise. Major Simpson rejoined from the 92nd Punjabis, but the men did not return until nearly a year later.

The next fortnight was a time of feverish activity, orders came to move to Jubbulpore before proceeding on field service, and this nearly doubled the work to be done. The battalion was divided into headquarters and fighting companies, and the depot, the latter of which was to remain at Jubbulpore.

The move to Jubbulpore took place on 21 October, the depot details following a few days later. Here the work of equipping the battalion went on apace, and on the 26th, a draft of two hundred men (half Sikhs and half P.M.s) arrived from our other linked battalion, the 72nd Punjabis, who were in Peshawar. This draft was a very good one, and many of them did exceptionally fine work in the field afterwards.

It had originally been decided that Captain Barrett was to command the depot, with Lieutenant Hodson to assist him, but a wire came from Simla to the effect that no L.A.R. officers were to be left behind in depots, so, to his intense disgust, 2nd Lieutenant Trevelyan, who had just joined the regiment, had to be left instead.

The work of mobilising a regiment for overseas service from the peace establishment is not so easy a task as it at first appears. Mobilisation Regulations and Army Tables, as they existed for the Indian Army before the war, were quite obsolete. Each class of regiment had a different strength for peace establishment. As all Burma Battalions were on the lower establishment, it threw things into hopeless confusion when we were ordered to mobilise to the same war strength as regiments of the higher establishment, while the practice of units purchasing their boots and clothing where and how they pleased did not help matters when the stocks existing in the country proved unequal to the demand. Some curious ideas appear to have existed during these early days in the minds of the higher authorities as to the scale of clothing necessary for a sepoy on service. Shirts were not an article of issue. He was supposed, apparently, to wear his coat next to his skin. The 'life' of one pair of socks was three months, and they were unreplaceable until that period had expired. Indeed, had it not been for the generosity of the various comfort funds raised in England, and of the relatives of officers in the regiment, who sent out large supplies of shirts and other necessaries, it is hard to know how the sepoy could have carried on at all during the first year of the war.

At 2 p.m. on 19 October, the regiment entrained at Jubbulpore for Karachi. On arrival at Gwalior, the officers were breakfasted, and the men feted by H.H. the Maharaja.

While passing through Delhi the regiment picked up, and took along with it, a party of reservists. These poor old men were in a terrible condition. Some had only the shreds of a coat on their backs. Others completely lacked the soles and heels of their boots. Many were so fat that they were with difficulty got into the carriages at all. None, from the expression on their faces, showed any apparent keenness for the job on hand. The Indian Army Reserve had never been mobilised in a wholesale manner before, and the old village patriarchs, while quite content to draw their monthly pittance for belonging to it, had overlooked the fact that they might be called upon for service.

On 2 November, the troop train arrived at Karachi, where Lieutenant J. V. Drought, 124th Baluchis, joined the battalion as Machine Gun Officer. The train drew up alongside the ship, SS *Takada*, and the day was spent in loading. The 24th Punjabis, and some Mule Corps details, shared the same ship, so that the men were most abominably crowded, though the officers were comfortable enough.

The following officers accompanied the regiment on service:-
  Lieutenant Colonel S. R. Stevens, C.O.
  Lieutenant Colonel J. H. Whitehead, O.C. No. IV. D.C.
  Major W. H. Simpson, O.C. No. II. D.C.
  Captain B. E. Morgan, O.C. No. I. D.C.
  Captain E. Cummings, Adjutant
  Lieutenant J. V. Drought, Machine Gun Officer
  Lieutenant R. J. K. Todd, O.C. No. III. D.C.
  Lieutenant W. S. Haycraft, Quartermaster
  Lieutenant V. C. L. Taylor
  2nd Lieutenant A. C. Pegg
  2nd Lieutenant S. S. Hodson
  Major Graham, I.M.S.

The battalion had originally been posted to Force F, and brigaded with the 7th Gurkhas and 24th Punjabis, but this was afterwards changed, and information arrived that the 93rd were detailed to Force E. Whether these two forces had originally been formed for different destinations is not generally known. They both went to Egypt and were the forerunners of what was ultimately termed the Egyptian Expeditionary Force, in which Force the regiment again served four years later.

The Karachi convoy collected together outside the harbour on the morning of 3 November, and later in the day met a similar convoy from Bombay. This now brought the total number of ships up to 48, with HMS *Swiftsure* as escort.

The journey was uneventful until Aden was reached. Here a considerable number of men who were suffering from itch had to be left behind.

On 16 November the convoy arrived off Suez, and, disembarking three days later, the regiment entrained, according to instructions, for Kantara. On arrival there at 5 p.m. the men detrained, and bivouacked on the west bank of the Canal. The next day everything was manhandled across the Canal, including 30 days' rations for the whole regiment, which had been drawn and brought with us from the SS *Takada*.

When we arrived, the 1-4th Gurkhas were occupying Kantara, but they left for France, and the 27th Punjabis and 93rd remained as garrison of the post.

Kantara was a very small and dirty place in the early days of the war. Our astonishment would have been great could our second arrival there some years later have been foreseen, when it had become the base of the whole of the British Army in Palestine. Great as were the changes wrought in Kantara during that time, they were, alas, no greater than the changes in the regiment itself.

In 1914, Kantara was just a filthy Bedouin village surrounding a minute mosque. While everything else has been swept away, the mosque still stands, testifying in a striking manner to the tolerant attitude of the British to other religions.

Around the village were a few solid buildings, which have also outlived the war. One of these is the police post, which was allotted to the 93rd as a mess and hospital. To the west the Quarantine House, afterwards Kantara Area Headquarters, stood where the road to Al Arish crossed the perimeter trenches. The 27th Punjabis took for their use some rest-houses on the outskirts of the village itself.

The post was commanded by Colonel Carey of the 27th Punjabis, and the 93rd held the southern face, while the 27th held the northern and eastern faces of the perimeter. (Sketch No. 1)

The time passed pleasantly and uneventfully at Kantara. By night the perimeter was occupied, and the days were spent in razing the village to the ground, and in digging the trenches and breastworks which formed the line of defence.

Every day at dawn one company went some three or four miles along the Al Arish road, acting as covering party and support to a camelry screen, and withdrawing at dusk.

Tents were not allowed owing to the fear of their showing up to the enemy, who, by the way, were still some two hundred miles away! Even if one could not get in touch with the enemy, everyone was keen in those days to imagine such a blissful state of affairs.

The chief difficulties at the time arose in connection with the men's rations. The scale allowed, while perhaps good enough for a three weeks' show on the North-West Frontier, was quite inadequate for a protracted campaign. Milk, sugar, green vegetables, and tobacco, were undreamt of by the S. and T. Corps, so all these necessities had to be supplied regimentally, and on payment, to the men.

Towards the middle of December, the 14th Sikhs arrived from Port

Said, and occupied the eastern face, with the Quarantine House as headquarters.

Christmas Day passed pleasantly. In the afternoon the 93rd were 'At Home' at regimental sports, and in the evening the 27th Punjabis gave a *Khattak* dance.[1]

On 9 January the 27th Punjabis and the 93rd were relieved at Kantara by the 69th and 89th Punjabis, who, with the 14th Sikhs, formed the 29th Brigade. Considerable reorganisation of the force in Egypt had taken place. The old Force E and Force F had disappeared, and two divisions, the 10th and 11th, had been formed in their place, the whole being known as the Indian Expeditionary Force E. Our move from Kantara was due to the necessity of collecting scattered units into their brigade areas in accordance with the above scheme.

On relief the two regiments entrained for Moascar, a new camp about a mile west of Ismailia, near the junction of the Suez and Port Said lines to Cairo. Here they joined the 31st Brigade of the 11th Division, composed as follows:-

    Brigadier - General Bingley
    Brigade Major - Captain H. C. Duncan, 9th Gurkhas
    Staff Captain - Captain F. A. Chamier, 33rd Punjabis
    Troops - 2nd Rajputs
           27th Punjabis
           93rd Burma Infantry
           128th Pioneers

As General Bingley was on the staff at Ismailia, he never actually took up his appointment, and Colonel Smith, of the 2nd Rajputs, officiated in his place.

The time at Moascar was again quite uneventful until the Turkish attack on the Canal on 3 February. Much to the regret of everyone in

---

[1] The *Khattak* dance is a martial dance traditional to the Pashtun tribes of Pakistan and Afghanistan. The dance is often performed at celebrations and at weddings (ed.).

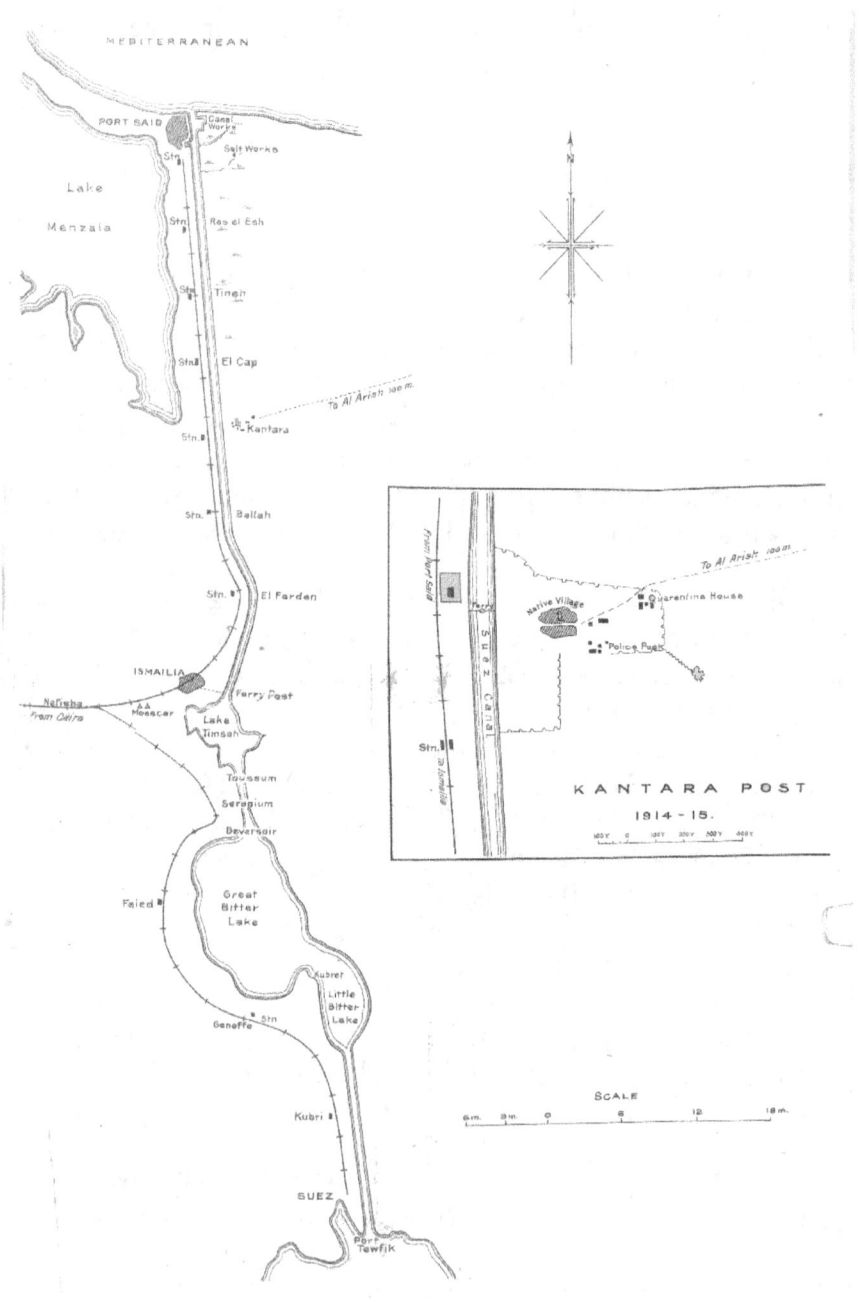

Sketch 1 The Suez Canal, 1914-1915

the regiment, things never became serious enough for the 93rd to be employed. At this time Captain Connellan, I.M.S., replaced Major Graham as M.O., and a draft arrived under the command of Captain Whitworth, 72nd Punjabis. The latter henceforth commanded No. III D.C. Three more officers also joined the regiment from the Ceylon Contingent, namely 2nd Lieutenants Thornton, Reyburn, and Bright.

Shortly after the failure of the Turkish attack on the Canal, No. II D.C. and the M.G. Section were suddenly ordered down to Kabret, at the junction of the Great and Little Bitter Lakes, as it was thought that the Turks might attempt a crossing there. This, however, never took place, but Kabret remained a more or less permanent detachment for the regiment. It was a delightful little place, with excellent bathing and fishing, while the lakes abounded with beds of quite good oysters.

On 21 March, orders were received for Lieutenant Thornton to join the 40th Pathans, who were passing through the Canal on their way to France, and next day the regiment was sent at an hour's notice to Kubri (about two stations north of Suez).

We arrived there at dusk, detrained, and bivouacked by the railway. Next day the 28th Brigade moved out to attack some Turks who had collected near the Canal, while the 93rd moved over to the east bank in support. In the evening the 28th Brigade returned, and half our battalion, under Colonel Whitehead, was sent to Suez.

Here happened an amusing incident. The detachment was dined by the 51st Sikhs, but Colonel Whitehead was unable to attend. The last member of the 93rd to arrive at dinner was Lieutenant Hodson – now known as 'Father', venerable in appearance, but not in rank. Treated with great respect, he was taken to be the C.O. and given the seat of honour. It was not for some time that our hosts discovered their mistake. After a few days the whole regiment returned to Moascar, and on 28 March moved to the Ferry Post at the northern end of Lake Timsah, where the 27th Punjabis camped on the east, and the 93rd on the west bank.

Beyond a plague of flies, and continuous fatigues for digging trenches in the sand, which invariably filled up again next day, the time again passed without incident, and on 3 May we entrained for Port Said, the remainder of the brigade going to Kantara.

At Port Said the regiment was split up. Headquarters, with Nos. III and IV D.C.s, encamped on the golf course, No. 1. D.C. went to the Canal Works on the east bank, and No. II D.C. to the Salt Works south-east of the town. Here we had the mortification of seeing the 29th Brigade embark for the Dardanelles.

While at Port Said, the 93rd won the Canal Defences Football Tournament, beating the 51st Sikhs in the finals, after a replay, by two goals to one. While practising for the tournament, Lieutenant Pegg had the misfortune to injure his leg badly, which afterwards necessitated his going to England for treatment.

At this time news came of the death of Captain F. L. Dyer in the Persian foothills. Captain Dyer had left the regiment just before the war to join the Persian Boundary Commission, and, while employed with them, was murdered by Arabs.

On 7 June the battalion was relieved by the 27th Punjabis at Port Said, and moved to Kantara, where the Quarantine House was used as headquarters and mess.

It had now become quite hot, and the period lives chiefly in one's memory through some decidedly unpleasant marches into the desert. The hot winds prevalent at this time of year were now at their worst, and during one of these marches several cases of heatstroke were experienced.

Shortly after our arrival at Kantara, No. 3194 Bur Singh murdered No. 3068 Nihal Singh, and No. 3208 Sadhu Singh, who were asleep in a dugout. After court-martial Bur Singh was shot and his body burnt. Here is a queer anomaly. Bur Singh, a murderer, was the only Sikh whose body was burnt during the whole war.

On 25 June, Colonel Whitehead was offered, and accepted, the command of a Territorial battalion in Gallipoli, and he departed shortly afterwards. Lieutenant Reyburn also left as a reinforcement to a regiment in the same theatre of war. At this time news came of the death of Major W. H. Ricketts in Gallipoli. When the war broke out Captain Ricketts was on leave in England. He was kept behind and made second in command of a service battalion of the Wiltshire Regiment in the 13th Division, with which he went to Gallipoli. He was killed leading his company in the first action in which they were engaged. Commonly called 'Nappy', Ricketts was one of the most popular officers in the regiment, and his loss was keenly felt by everyone.

While at Kantara, Lieutenant Pestonji relieved Captain Connellan as M.O., and three more officers joined from the Ceylon Contingent, namely, 2nd Lieutenants Martin, Owen, and Hobday. The first two only stayed a few weeks, after which they were transferred to the British service.

During July our headquarters was moved back to the police post, where we had lived on our first arrival at Kantara. The 27th Punjabis took over the Quarantine House after being relieved by the 128th Pioneers at Port Said.

While here the regiment was split up into small detachments stretching from near Ballah in the south to Tineh in the north (Sketch No. 1). The only irksome part of this detachment life was at night, when posts had to maintain communication with each other by frequent patrols along the east bank.

The authorities were in perpetual fear that the enemy might creep up at night and launch a mine in the canal. Could they have sunk a ship in the fairway it would, of course, have severed our communications with India and the East, until the obstruction was removed. One mine was successfully launched, and damaged a ship in the Bitter Lakes, but luckily the vessel was able to put in to the side, and the canal passage was left clear.

Every night planks of wood some six feet in length were dragged along the east bank for the whole extent of the canal. These left a clear track of sand behind them, which was examined for footprints in the morning by patrols sent out from the different posts.

The regiment had now been 10 months on service, and had only heard the noise of battle from a distance. There seemed little hope of the Turks making a second attempt on the canal, and the chances of getting into the thick of things seemed to become more and more remote.

Judge, then, our delight when one morning, soon after breakfast, the brigade major came with the news that the 27th and 33rd Punjabis, and 93rd Burma Infantry, had been ordered to France.

Excitement was intense, and every day that elapsed before departure dragged like an age. Finally, the 6th Jats and 41st Dogras arrived from France, and, having exchanged our low velocity for the high velocity rifles of the latter regiment, we embarked at Port Said on the SS *Erinpura* with half the 33rd Punjabis on 14 September.

PART II

FRANCE

Chapter II
France, September, 1915 – December, 1915

The voyage to France was a very pleasant one. The ship was not overcrowded, and beyond the continual darkened lights, and perpetual fear of submarines, it passed without incident.

The *Erinpura* arrived at Marseilles on 18 September, a morning of rain and mist. Here orders were received to disembark and proceed by special troop train at 5 p.m. that night.

The ship drew up alongside an enormous ordnance dump, and the day was spent in re-equipping the men with serge and warm underclothing, and in replacing our Mk.VI. by Mk.VII. S.A.A. This feat, which was accomplished in six hours, testifies to the efficiency of the Ordnance Department in France. More was done during those six hours than would have been possible in six weeks in India before the war.

During the day, Captain Barrett, who had arrived previously with a draft that was waiting at the Base Depot, rejoined the regiment. Captain Barrett had previously handed over command of the depot to Captain Alves – an officer who had left the regiment a few years before the war to join the Burma Civil Commission and on arrival assumed command of No. IV. D.C.

All men surplus to the war establishment were left with Lieutenant Hodson at the Base Depot, and everything being finally complete and the train loaded, we left Marseilles at about 6 p.m.

Of the journey to the front, little is worth recording beyond the hospitality of the habitants, and the pleased surprise of the men at their first view of a European countryside. It was otherwise a long and tedious journey, and took three days before arrival at our destination.

Our first sign of the war in France was heard on the afternoon of 21 September, when the train arrived at Chocques, near Bethune. Here an otherwise peaceful scene was ominously disturbed by the rumbling of guns, and the clusters of shell-puffs round some scouting aeroplanes.

At Merville, which was reached at about 9 p.m., orders were received to detrain at Beaupré, some two miles further on.

Here a divisional transport officer awaited the regiment, and handed over all the 1st and 2nd Line Transport. He also indicated a farm a half-mile away where billets could be obtained. The men bivouacked in a field, while the officers slept in a hay-loft. Information had been received at Merville that the regiment was posted to the 19th (Dehra Dun) Brigade of the 7th (Meerut) Division. The brigade was composed as follows:-

    Brigadier - General Harvey
    Brigade Major - Major Anderson, 59th Rifles
    Staff Capitan - Captain Thornton, 24th Punjabis
    Troops - 1st Seaforth Highlanders
        2-2nd Gurkha Rifles
        1-9th Gurkha Rifles
        93rd Burma Infantry
        4th Seaforth Highlanders (attached)

On 23 September, the regiment was inspected by General Anderson, the Corps Commander, who was greatly impressed by the bearing and stature of the men.

While at Beaupré Farm, batches of officers were sent up to visit the front line trenches. An inkling was obtained at this time that an

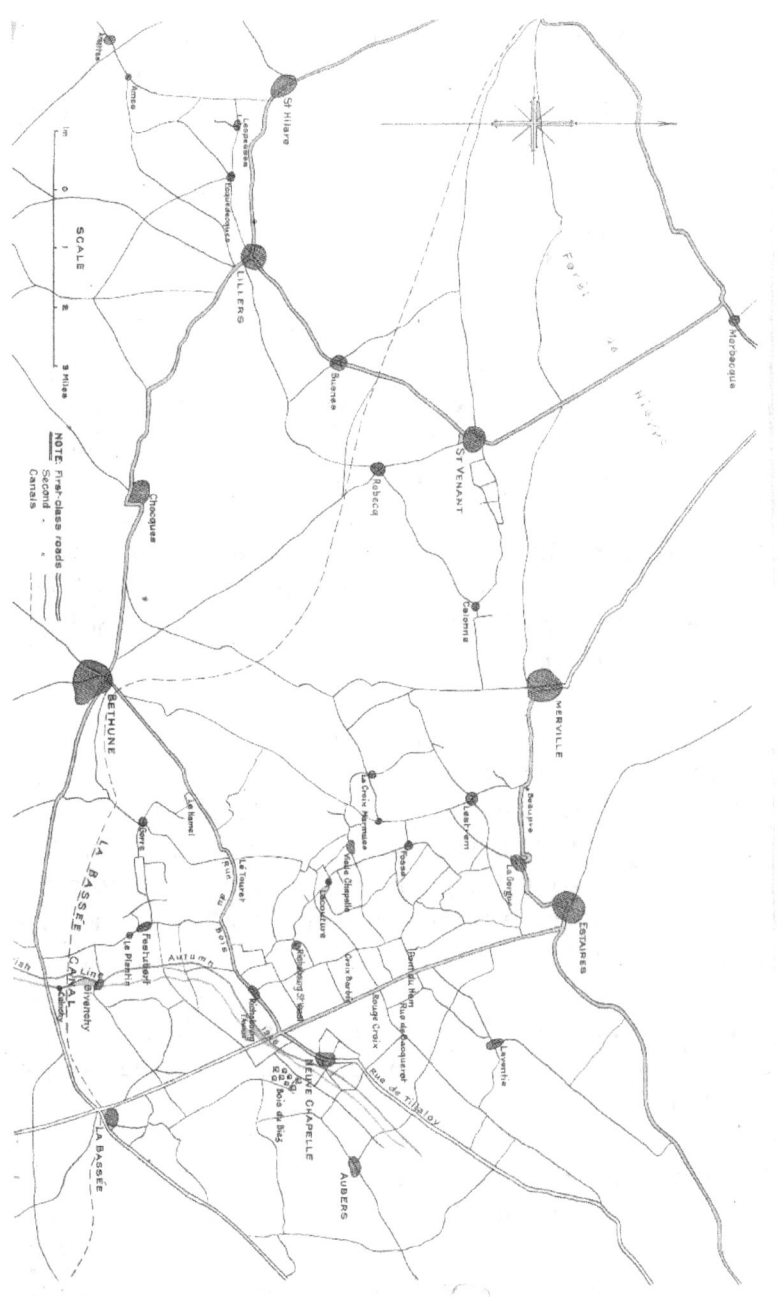

Sketch 2, France – The Indian Corps Front 1915

offensive on a very large scale was impending. Surplus kits were dumped near Merville, and on 23 September orders came to march to a support post, just north of Pont du Hem, on the Estaires – La Bassée road.

That day, complete ordnance equipment, from machine guns to gas masks, was drawn at Estaires, and delivered to the regiment at about midnight.

The regiment remained in this post until the morning of the attack (25 September). The offensive was to stretch from Loos in the south to near Armentières in the north. On our divisional front the 20th and 21st Brigades were to attack, with our brigade in reserve.

By this time, bombardments were almost incessant, but throughout the night of 24/25 September, the intensity of it was awful. At 8 a.m. on the 25th, orders were received to march to the support trenches at the Rue de Bacquerot. (Sketch No. 2.)

The attack up to this time appeared to be going favourably, and large batches of German prisoners and wounded could be seen coming in. During the afternoon the regiment moved up to the front line through many miles of communication trenches. The division on our left, however, had come to grief, and when orders were received to return to Rue de Bacquerot, to make room for the attacking troops who were retiring to our front line, it became obvious that the attack had failed.

The night of 25/26 was spent in the open, with no shelter, and under a continuous downpour. It was only made bearable by the arrival at midnight of food and a liberal rum ration.

On 26 September, we relieved the 21st Brigade in the front line near Neuve Chapelle. This brigade had been badly cut up during the preceding day. Pretty severe rifle fire was maintained throughout the first night, during which we suffered over 20 casualties. The weather was vile throughout the whole of our first spell in the trenches, during which the time was chiefly spent in recovering the wounded and killed lying in front of our wire. When relieved on the evening of the 28th, it took some companies 12 hours to extricate themselves from the mud, and arrive back at billets at Vieille Chapelle. It was 10 a.m. next morning before No.1 D.C. appeared, too tired to carry anything except a half-empty rum jar.

After a few days' rest at Vieille Chapelle, our brigade relieved another brigade in the Givenchy sector, the 2-2nd Gurkhas and Seaforths being in the front line, and the 1-9th Gurkhas and 93rd in support, behind the villages of Festubert and Le Plantin.

Beyond a period of complete paralysis on the part of the mess cook, caused by the consumption of a considerable quantity of discarded mess gin, nothing of note happened until 6 October, when the 93rd relieved the 2-2nd Gurkhas in the front line just north of Givenchy, remaining there until the 21st. The weather was distinctly better during this, our second, visit to the trenches, and the men were rapidly getting inured to the local conditions.

While we were in this sector, Lieutenant J. G. Swaine joined the regiment, but, being comparatively well off in regular officers, two had to be sent away. Captain Whitworth left to join the 69th Punjabis, and Lieutenant Todd the 58th Rifles.

The only important event that occurred before our relief was a sham attack, preceded by a smoke barrage, on 15 October. This naturally led to considerable retaliation, and a fairly heavy bombardment.

The regiment was relieved during the night of the 21st, and marched to reserve billets at Richebourg St Vaast, which wretched village was very much the worse for wear. It was quite deserted, and there was not a whole house left in the place. This period is memorable for the reappearance of the cheerful face of 'Father' (Lieutenant Hodson) who rejoined from the Marseilles Base Depot.

On 24 October the regiment moved to rest billets at Calonne-sur-Lys. This was a long march, and the men arrived in an exhausted condition after their sedentary life in the trenches, only to find that next day two hundred men had to return to Richebourg St. Vaast for duty as a working party. At Calonne-sur-Lys we slept in beds for the first time since our arrival in France. Our time was chiefly spent in improving the regimental bombers. Bombs had not been issued in Egypt, so that our battalion was naturally somewhat backward in this respect, especially as there were about 12 kinds of bomb to master. A certain amount of adjustment in B.O.'s took place at this time. Captain Cummings took over No. III D.C., Lieutenant Haycraft becoming adjutant, and Lieutenant Hodson quartermaster.

On 28 October the brigade was paraded for inspection by H.M. the King. After waiting many hours in the intense cold and rain, news arrived that the inspection was cancelled. It appears that the King had a severe accident on his way to the parade ground. Rumour had it that our brigade was detailed for an impending attack, and that this was cancelled, the accident being taken as a bad omen.

About this time news was received that the Indian Corps was shortly to leave France for another theatre of operations. Of course, tongues soon began to wag, and opinions as to our destination varied between Salonika, Egypt, and Mesopotamia.

On 2 November the 19th Brigade took over the front line trenches opposite Richebourg St Vaast from the 20th Brigade, the 1-9th Gurkhas and 93rd being in the front line.

During this turn in the trenches Major Simpson was in command, Colonel Stevens having gone on short leave to England.

It had been raining heavily before the regiment took over the line, and continued while they were in it, so that the trenches were in an abominable condition. The front line and supports were running streams varying from one to three feet deep. The only communication between Battalion Headquarters and the front line was down a trench waist deep, and containing frequent holes over a man's depth. The headquarter's mess was in a dugout in which the top of the table was only a few inches above water level. While seated at it, one's legs were immersed up to the knee. If the water was left undisturbed, there was a quarter-of-an-inch of ice on it in the morning.

In these not very ideal conditions the regiment spent six days, by which time the men's feet were in a pitiable condition. It was no uncommon sight to see a man's foot swollen to the size of his head, while some had to have their feet amputated afterwards. The reader must remember that they had been standing in ice-cold water for 144 hours, without gum-boots or any other protection.

The condition of the ground made the rationing arrangements very difficult. While the regiment was in the front line rations were brought up by the quartermaster after dark. Up to within about two miles they came on carts, after which trolley lines were laid down as far as Battalion Headquarters. Here rations were distributed and carried off by company fatigues. As often as not there were large quantities of revetting material, stores, and clothing, et cetera, to bring up, and, as the trollies invariably took a fiendish delight in parting company from their rails, the quartermaster's night was usually a weary and blasphemous one. The position of the trolley lines, and the usual time of the arrival of rations, were of course known to the Germans. Hence as a rule matters were made less easy by a machine gun playing up and down the line.

On relief, nearly half the regiment had to be transported to billets at Croix Marmuse by motor, as their frostbitten feet rendered them quite incapable of marching more than a few hundred yards. After one night at Croix Marmuse we were taken to rest billets at Morbecque on motor buses. It was pitiful to see many men crawling on all fours through the village street towards their billets. It was not until a month later that the men's feet were really fit for marching.

The country people around Morbecque were very different from those further south. Being near the Belgian frontier, they were of a mongrel type, and almost looked on one with hostility. Formerly nothing could have been more friendly than the attitude of the inhabitants towards the sepoy, but here they did all they could in the gentle art of obstruction. The sepoy, indeed, must have appeared a weird creature to the local French people, with his way of standing naked in the open to bathe, of walking down the village street with his nether limbs clad only in his drawers, and of never accepting the first price of an article as final.

On 13 November, the brigade marched to fresh billets via the Forét de Nieppe, the 93rd being quartered in the village of Lespesses. This was quite a long march, and the men suffered considerably on account of their feet.

While at Lespesses, Lieutenant Swaine went sick with a bad knee. During this period the Indian Corps was gradually moving south, on their way to another theatre of operations, and it was known that our turn would soon come. On 18 November, our billets were changed to the village of Ameites, where Lieutenant Todd rejoined from the 58th Rifles. Five days later the regiment entrained at Lillers for Marseilles.

At Marseilles we stayed at Camp Sante, some three miles west of the town, and found awaiting us the original draft that had been sent to the 92nd Punjabis at the beginning of the war.

Our embarkation was delayed owing to the fact that large bodies of troops were at this time proceeding through Marseilles to Salonika.

On 3 December, Battalion Headquarters and the left wing, together with the 69th Punjabis, having embarked the afternoon before, left Marseilles on the SS *Taroba*, while the right wing, with the 1-9th Gurkhas, left on the SS *Cawdor Castle* two days later. Lieutenant Drought was left behind in charge of the transport and officers' chargers, which were to embark on another ship.

Both vessels took the same course, first calling at Toulon, and then proceeding via Corsica and Sardinia to Malta. From here the course took a wide sweep round to Alexandria, and then to Port Said.

The Taroba, though sighting a sinking ship, did not encounter a submarine, but the Cawdor Castle had quite an exciting escape. A submarine put some 30 shells over her, but the skilful manoeuvring of her commander avoided a direct hit. The first submarine had, however, driven her on to a second one, but the ship's gun crew got on to it with such precision that it must have been knocked out. Anyhow, it never appeared again. The men fell in and behaved splendidly without the slightest excitement.

It was not until our arrival at Port Said that it was known what our ultimate destination was to be. Here orders were received for the 69th Punjabis to disembark, and for the 93rd Burma Infantry to proceed to Basra.

Application was made, and consented to, for the right wing to tranship to the Taroba. This was effected at Suez. The whole regiment was now together, and the voyage onwards, without fear of submarines, was very pleasant.

PART III

MESOPOTAMIA

Chapter III
First Battle of Hannah, 21 January 1916

At Aden, orders were received to push on at top speed, and on New Year's Day, the *Taroba* arrived outside the Shatt al Arab, but was unable to cross the Bar. So, on the first day of the most eventful year of the regiment's history, the low-lying shores of the land were sighted, whose memory must ever be as a nightmare to those that survived its long campaigns. Of the 11 British officers who disembarked from the SS *Taroba*, only five were alive four months later; while in the same period the battalion strength was reduced from 735 to 96.

During the morning of 3 January, the regiment disembarked at Margil, then nothing more than a minute ration dump in a clearing among the palm trees.

Very little definite news from the front was obtainable at Basra. It was certain that General Townshend's force had suffered a reverse at Ctesiphon, and had retreated to Kut al Amara, where the Turks had cut him off. The general opinion, however, was that this was only a momentary check, and that the advance on Baghdad would soon commence again. Alas for our optimism! It was not until 15 months later that the British entered Baghdad, many months of which contained as uncomfortable and disheartening warfare as has been seen in any theatre of operations during the war.

While at Margil, Lieutenant Trevelyan rejoined from the depot. Owing to the shortage in river transport, some regiments were marching upstream. We, however, were lucky enough to go by boat – especially lucky in our ideas then, as we thought the regiments that marched would be too late for the entry into Baghdad.

On 7 January the battalion embarked on the *P2*, with its two attendant barges, and proceeded up stream.

On the way, news was received that the operations for the relief of Townshend at Kut had opened with the Battle of Sheikh Saad. At Amara we were visited by Major Haughton of the 92nd Punjabis, who had been wounded in the battle, and later commanded our regiment. Orders were also received for us to proceed to Ali Gharbi for disembarkation, but on arrival there at midnight, a voice hailed us from the bank with instructions to push on at full steam for Sheikh Saad.

The *P2* arrived at Sheikh Saad (Sketch No. 3) on the morning of 13 January, passing the old battlefield just below the town. As the boat rounded the last bend in the river, the sound of gunfire in the distance was distinctly audible, where the battle afterwards known as the Battle of the Wadi was proceeding.

We disembarked from the *P2*, and spent a busy day taking over and distributing transport. Instructions were received to send on all transport at an early hour next morning to Orah, and for the regiment to follow on receipt of orders.

That night outposts were put out along the left bank, and, at dawn, Lieutenant Hodson took on the transport. The regiment marched at 11 a.m., with the exception of No. 1 D.C., under Captain Morgan, which remained as escort to the G.O.C. on board the Mejidiyeh.

The situation in Mesopotamia at the time was as follows. Having boxed up the 6th Division under General Townshend in Kut, the Turks held them with a small containing force, and had pushed the bulk of their troops downstream to meet our relief column. This relieving force was commanded by General Aylmer, and had originally concentrated at Ali Gharbi. It was to consist of the Indian Corps from France, with the 35th and 36th Brigades attached.

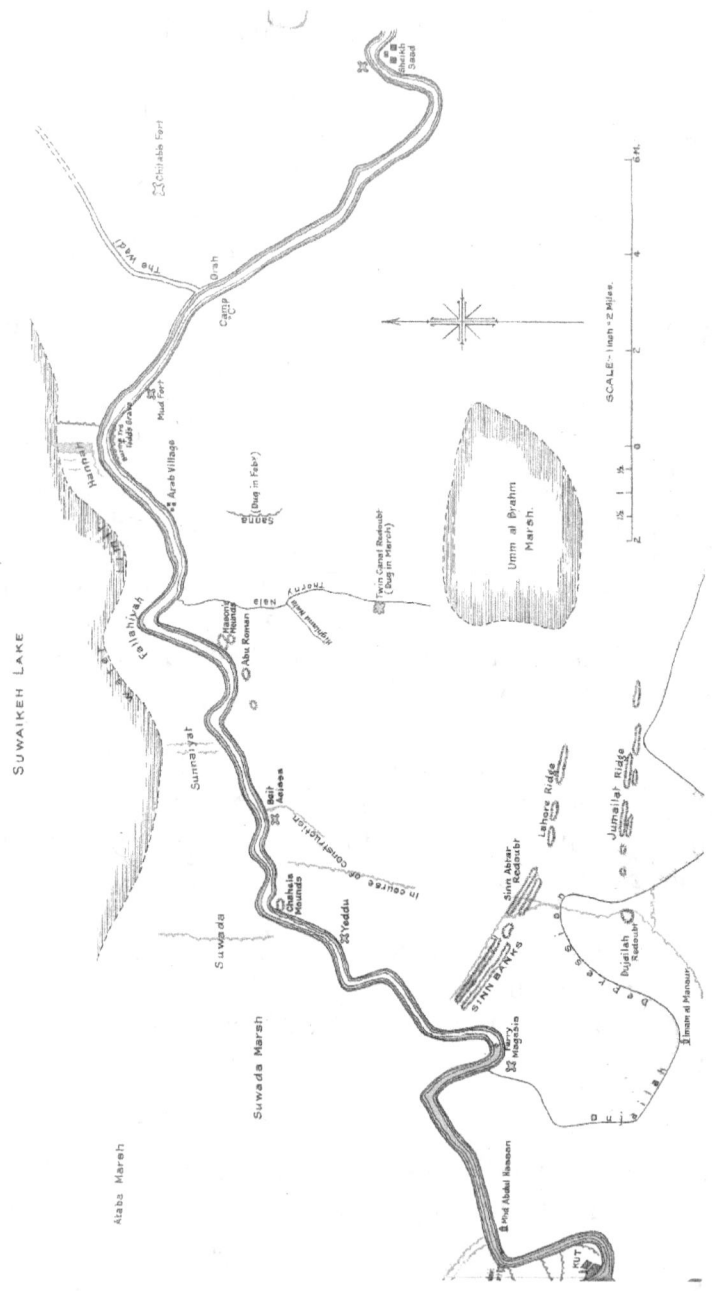

Sketch 3 Skeikh Saad – Kut, January – March 1916
Chapters III and IV

The fact that most of our fighting troops on the Tigris were shut up in Kut had caused a very grave situation at the time. To meet this situation many regiments were hurriedly dispatched from Egypt to Mesopotamia, while the Indian Corps, coming on later, dropped a similar number of regiments in Egypt.

It was decided to reform the 7th (Meerut) Division first, and this division, therefore, when reformed, consisted for the most part of the hitherto unblooded regiments from Egypt, who arrived before those from France. When ready, the 7th Division advanced from Ali Gharbi to commence the operations for the relief of Kut, and met and drove back the Turks on two occasions, firstly at Sheikh Saad on 7 January, and secondly at the Wadi on 13 January.

A glance at Sketch No. 3 will show the reader that these two battles were really only what might be called covering actions on the part of the Turk. He could have had no hope of holding us up in either position, as in both cases his left flank was in the air, and the flank, as everyone knows, is always the vulnerable point. Having, therefore, just extricated himself at the last moment in both battles, he retired on to his main defensive position at Hannah.

This position at Hannah was an exceptionally strong one. The frontage was short, and both flanks secure, one being on the river, and the other on the impassable Suwaikeh Marsh. In this way the position constituted an almost impregnable defile, and one that could only be taken by frontal assault. Having ousted him from the Wadi, the 7th Division followed up the Turk, and dug in before Hannah. This was the state of affairs on 14 January, when the regiment marched into Orah.

Ours was among the first of the regiments from France to arrive, and with the advent of these it became possible to reform the 3rd (Lahore) Division, which, with the 7th, had constituted the Indian Corps in France. It was decided that the 3rd Division should reform on the right bank, on which bank we had no troops at the time, and ours was actually the first regiment of the 3rd Division to cross to the bank on which all future operations of the division took place.

On the right bank the enemy's main position was at Sinn Banks (Sketch No. 3). These ancient canal banks were very strongly entrenched, and, though normally only lightly held, could be quickly reinforced from the Turkish General Reserve at Kut by means of the ferry at Magasis. In front of this position they had commenced work on the Beit Aeissa and Chahela trenches, and had established picquets at Mason's Mounds and Arab Village, while cavalry patrols scoured the country southwards to the Umm al Brahm Marsh.

Before perusing the account of the operations to follow, the reader should bear in mind the local conditions of Mesopotamia, which had a direct influence on the campaign, both tactically, and by causing the most acute discomfort to the troops engaged.

With the exception of the artificial banks of the Sinn Canal, and a few sand hills along the edge of the river, there was not a rise in the ground between Sheikh Saad and Kut. Neither was there a tree or any undergrowth over a few feet high. The ground was literally as flat as a pancake. Consider the effect of this on attacking troops opposed by good rifle and machine gun fire. They were mown down much as corn is mown by a scythe.

It had come as a relief to the Indian Corps to hear that they were leaving France, with the monotonous trench life, and the mole-like existence it entailed. Straight-forward, open warfare, they thought, such as they had practised and learnt in peace time, would now be the order of the day. Little did they realise the toll of their ranks that would be taken by an advance over some 2,000 yards of flat, illimitable mud, against a well-armed and disciplined enemy – a toll which made open warfare prohibitive, and a reversion to trench warfare necessary. No longer were our troops to meet the Arab levies who had opposed Townshend's gallant little force. The true Anatolian Turk from Gallipoli was now appearing in Mesopotamia for the first time.

Normally the rainfall in Mesopotamia is not excessive, but in the spring of 1916 it exceeded all records, at the worst covering the ground with a sheet of water, and at the best leaving it a slippery sea of almost impassable mud.

The supply of rations was very difficult. Food was cooked at Camp C, and from there taken by carts or pack mules to the regiment in the line. This necessitated a daily trek for the quartermaster, varying from 6 to 20 miles. The men consequently never had a warm meal, while the officers got nothing but biscuits and bully.

Tents, except for those near G.H.Q., were unknown. One's normal habitation was a scrape in the ground covered by a waterproof sheet. As it was a war of movement, one seldom slept in the same place many days running. A hole scraped in the water-saturated ground, as described above, does not present a very cosy picture of a home.

There were no canteens, which in later days followed the infantry as soon as a battlefield was cleared. Cigarettes, milk, and sugar, et cetera (so dear to the sepoy's heart), were only obtainable through a very precarious supply from Arab dealers at Orah, who made exorbitant charges. Ten 'Red Lamp' cigarettes, normally one anna, fetched anything up to a rupee, while milk, sugar, and other necessities, were at equally scandalous prices.[2]

There is little exaggeration in saying that the attempt to relieve Kut in the spring of 1916 constituted one of the most trying operations undertaken by the British Army during the war, leaving one's morale, as it did, under the stigma of defeat, in a most abject condition. It is necessary to add the opinion that no troops in the world, in similar circumstances, could have accomplished more than the Kut Relief Force did.

After a miserable wet night on outpost without shelter at Orah, the regiment crossed the Tigris on the morning of 15 January, Colonel

---

[2] In Imperial India one rupee was made up of 16 anna (ed.).

Stevens having received orders to command a column consisting of the 93rd and the 1-1st Gurkhas, who were just arriving upstream, and to seize the Mud Fort. The Mud Fort was unoccupied, and we took up an outpost line starting on the river bank about a mile north-west of the fort, and sweeping round in a south-easterly direction. The 1-1st Gurkhas afterwards continued this line to opposite Orah, behind which screen the camp known as Camp C sprang up, in which the 3rd Division was gradually being concentrated.

General Aylmer, G.O.C. Relief Force, having been informed by General Townshend that the Kut food supply was running short, decided to attack the Hannah position. To help the attack by enfilade fire from the right bank the 93rd were ordered to construct what were afterwards known as Burma Trenches (Sketch No. 3), and occupy them the night preceding the attack.

During the few days before the attack, the weather was very wet, and the river almost overflowed its banks. The flood was so great that the bridge at Orah broke, and, in consequence, for two days we got no rations. Officers were reduced to boiling the dregs of discarded bully beef tins with water in order to make soup.

The first Battle of Hannah, originally ordered for 18 January, was postponed several times, and did not actually take place until the morning of the 21st. Meantime the 1-9th Gurkhas had seized Arab Village.

During the night of 20/21, the 93rd dug and occupied Burma Trenches. An intermittent bombardment of 24 hours' duration culminated in intense fire at 7.45 a.m., on the 21st. Aided by this, and by our enfilade fire, the 7th Division entered the Turkish lines. Bodies of Turks retreating across the open were caught by our fire, and severely dealt with, and by 10 a.m. the position appeared to be in our hands. As our ammunition was running very short, a message was sent to Lieutenant Todd, who was acting as Regimental Transport Officer, to bring up the 1st Line S.A.A. Meantime a steady downpour had commenced, and sounds of bombing from the trenches in front showed that everything was not going according to plan. At the same time the enemy, exasperated by our fire, turned a considerable portion of their attention on to us.

Suddenly the 7th Division could be seen evacuating the Turkish trenches, and retreating in complete disorder to their own lines, pursued by bodies of Turks.

The enemy fire on us increased in volume, and the S.A.A. mules, now arriving with Lieutenant Todd across some 400 yards of open country, drew a hail of bullets. Five mules were instantly killed, and, as they were tied in threes, this caused a stampede. No. 2828 Sepoy Bhan Singh ran into the open, and collecting a few men, managed to unload all the ammunition. He afterwards received the I.D.S.M. for his gallantry. This incident lost us 13 mules.

Lieutenant Todd, famous for his slow and methodical manner, languidly strolled across the open to join his company. He appeared to be absolutely unaware of the intense fire he was under. As soon as he reached the trench he pitched headfirst into it, hit in three places. He died at 3 p.m. in considerable pain, and was buried within 10 yards of where he was wounded. About this time Captain Barrett was hit through the shoulder, and Subadar Major Mahomed Baksh through the shoulder-blade. Both continued to carry on their duties until the evening. Jemadar Saiyed Zaman was also very seriously wounded through the stomach. This Indian Officer never recovered from his wound, and died some nine months later.

The downpour continued all day, and the fact that the attack had been a hopeless failure did not tend to raise our spirits. In the evening orders were received for the 93rd to return to the Mud Fort. The steady rain had reduced the ground to a spongy sea of mud, and it took several hours to cover the odd two miles of country, every step of which imperilled one's vertical position. On arrival we were told to send one double-company back, and the unfortunate No. III D.C. under Captain Cummings, had to return to Burma Trenches.

The remainder of the regiment, however, also obtained little rest, for Nos. II and IV D.C.s were sent to link up picquets with No. I D.C. which, before the attack, had been sent on outpost, facing south-west, some two miles from the Mud Fort. This was an impossible thing to accomplish; the bearing of No. I D.C. was unknown; it was raining hard, and the ground was already ankle-deep in mud and water. Into this hopeless quagmire wandered the two double- companies, which soon lost themselves, and spent a miserable night standing up in the slush, a more comfortable position than sitting down.

At midnight orders were received that the attack would be renewed at dawn, and that the 93rd were to return to the old trenches before 6 a.m. Runners were sent to the various companies with orders to close independently on Burma Trenches before dawn, and, by the merest good fortune, the runners found their companies. Luckily the rain ceased before daybreak, but it was a very bedraggled and miserable regiment which found itself reassembled in Burma Trenches next morning.

During the night our wounded had passed through an agonising time – though no worse than those of the 7th Division on the other bank. It is unnecessary to expand on the scandals of the hospital arrangements in Mesopotamia in early 1916, as they are already well known. It will be sufficient to say that the ambulances had not accompanied their divisions from France; that the nearest hospital to us was six miles away, without any means of transport there; and that our wounded, sodden with rain, and numbed with cold, received no more attention than is possible in a Regimental Aid Post which possesses no shelter, until next day.

The attack on the 22nd did not come off – indeed, anyone could have seen that the condition of the ground would not admit it. Instead there was an armistice, and at 11 a.m. the white flag left the Turkish and our lines, and parties were sent out to collect the wretched wounded, who had been lying out for 24 hours. At 1 p.m. hostilities were renewed, but both sides were tired and dispirited, and by a kind of mutual consent not another shot was fired for the remainder of the day.

The weather now took a turn for the better, and the next few days were more pleasant; sniping competitions with the enemy lending a zest to the proceedings. A certain number of casualties were suffered each day, besides those lost on the 21st, chiefly owing to men going into the open to collect brushwood.

Subadar Major Mahomed Baksh, who refused to go to hospital, was still with the regiment, but Captain Barrett, whose wound was more serious, had gone down stream.

Our stay in Burma Trenches was a particularly trying time for the quartermaster, Lieutenant Hodson. The mud was so thick that even the A.T. cart was defeated, and rations had to be brought all the way from Camp C on pack mules by night.

At this time news was received that Lieutenant Pegg, who, it will be remembered, had left the regiment in Egypt, and had been reported missing from the SS *Persia*, was alive and well.

On 27 January, instructions came to return to Camp C, and we evacuated Burma Trenches during the night. During the next day our bivouacs were moved four times, the third time finding us back at Mud Fort. The regiment had just settled in for the night there, and food was being prepared, when orders were received to return forthwith to Burma Trenches, which we had left less than 24 hours before. We were, however, getting inured to orders and counter-orders, and by 9 p.m. were once more ensconced in Burma Trenches.

Our third stay in these trenches brought us up to 2 February, when Nos. I, III, and IV D.C.s retired during the night to Mud Fort, leaving No. II D.C., under Major Simpson, and the machine gun section, under Lieutenant Bright, behind.

The same day we had to march out to support the 33rd Cavalry, who were moving south-west to recover the body of a British officer who had been killed while on patrol. The regiment came under considerable long-range fire, but suffered no casualties.

The only other event of note that occurred at Mud Fort was the formal permission granted by the G.O.C. 3rd Division to Captain Morgan to grow a beard, he being the only British officer who could produce a growth sufficient to disguise him as a Sikh.

During the night of 4 February, a patrol of No. III D.C., under Lance Naik Mahomed Ghani disappeared. At the conclusion of hostilities, when prisoners of war were returned, Sepoy Samundar Khan, who was one of the patrol, and the only one to survive, stated that they had been caught by Turkish cavalry.

On the 12th the regiment was relieved at Mud Fort and Burma Trenches by the 2nd Rajputs, and marched to Camp C, where the brigade was collected together for the first time.

The 93rd were posted to the 9th (Sirhind) Brigade, and not the 7th Brigade as had been originally decided. The composition of the brigade was as follows:-
      Brigadier – General Campbell, 89th Punjabis
      Brigade Major – Captain Hamilton, M.C., Connaught Rangers
      Staff Captain – Captain Reinhold, 27th Punjabis
      Troops – 1st Bn Highland Light Infantry
            93rd Burma Infantry
            1-1st Gurkha Rifles
            1-9th Gurkha Rifles

The division was under the command of General Keary, and the other brigades were composed as follows. 7th Brigade – Connaught Rangers, 27th and 89th Punjabis, and 128th Pioneers. 8th Brigade – Manchesters, 2nd Rajputs, 47th Sikhs, and 59th Rifles.

Chapter IV,
Battle of Duyar Lanh, 8 March, 1916

The brigade remained at Camp C for some time, during which they marched out every day to dig the Sanna position. This trench system, though never actually needed, was intended as a stepping-off place for the operations which were to follow. The brigade would march out in diamond formation, and, under the protection of a covering party, work on the position all day, and return to Camp C in the evening. These digging operations were generally unmolested, but one day a covering party of No.1 D.C. was charged by Arab cavalry. The result was a large expenditure of ammunition, but little of blood.

It gradually became evident that preparations were in progress for a big move on the right bank, though the exact nature of it was still a matter of conjecture. These preparations were soon complete, and at dusk on 21 February, the 3rd Division marched from Camp C and congregated in bivouacs at the Sanna position, with orders to be ready to march at 1 a.m. The division did not arrive at Sanna until after dark, and by the time we had settled into bivouacs, and the men had had their food, there was little time left for sleep.

At midnight operation orders were issued. The brigade was to march to Abu Roman in double-column of fours, the 93rd and 1-9th Gurkhas leading, and the H.L.I. and 1-lst Gurkhas behind, while the 93rd were to supply an advanced guard of one double-company (No. I D.C. under Captain Morgan). It was a weary night march, interspersed with long halts in order to allow the machine guns, which were manhandled, to keep up on the nala-intersected ground. After going some distance, a certain amount of wild firing came from the front and left flank, and battalions changed formation to quarter-columns. The pace became even slower now that this unwieldy formation was adopted.

At about an hour before dawn, rapid fire was opened by the advanced guard. This at the time caused considerable consternation behind, as it was not known whether it was our own or enemy fire. There is nothing so disconcerting as to hear rapid fire by night, and not to know whence it comes.

The advanced guard had run into about a dozen Arab cavalry. They succeeded in killing one, but the remainder careered down the right flank of the 1-9th Gurkhas, and, as far as is known, escaped unscathed.

A flank guard under Captain Cummings, sent off to the left, also met and dispersed a patrol of Arab cavalry.

Soon afterwards day broke, and we found ourselves within a few hundred yards of Abu Roman mounds, with the 8th Brigade on our right. In pursuance of operation orders, the H.L.I. and 1-1st Gurkhas remained at Abu Roman, while the 93rd and 1-9th Gurkhas continued to advance along the right bank to capture a reputed fort in the next bend of the river.

As day broke, the Turkish camp on the left bank, in rear of their position at Hannah, became clearly visible, and the guns that had been brought with our column opened fire. The result was wonderful. The whole of the gun-teams and transport animals of the Turkish force at Hannah broke, and fled in the wildest confusion. Horses, mules, and bullocks, saddled and unsaddled, hemmed in on the south by the river, and on the north by the marsh, careered madly across our front at a range of not more than two miles. The result was pleasing to us, and must have been correspondingly annoying to the Turk, but the tactical situation remained unchanged. The Turk did not budge from Hannah.

This bend of the river was that across which Townshend had thrown his bridge when he transferred his force to the left bank in the Battle of Kut al Amara, and most people supposed that the object of our expedition was to do likewise, and so surround the Turks at Hannah. Had we been able during the early morning, on arrival at Abu Roman, to force a crossing of the Tigris, and so take Hannah in reverse, there is little doubt that the whole history of the campaign would have been altered. The force of the current may have prohibited it, or there may have been other reasons that prevented the powers-that-be from attempting it, but to the mind of an ordinary regimental officer, it appeared to be a golden opportunity missed.

The advance of the 1-9th Gurkhas and 93rd continued in artillery formation, and came under fire of a battery of small calibre near Beit Aeissa. This did little damage. The fort we were to capture turned out to be unoccupied and in ruins, and both regiments put out a picquet line from the river bank southwards, with the left flank refused. The enemy shelling was now getting more serious, and Captain Morgan's life was undoubtedly saved by the pack he carried on his back. Our picquet line had no sooner been dug than, as invariably happens on such occasions, orders came to alter our alignment. We stayed in this outpost line some days, our only casualties being caused by snipers on the other bank.

On the 23rd a most amusing incident occurred, when a herd of goats came wandering over our picquets. The thought of fresh meat was too much for the men, and with one accord both regiments leapt from their trenches under the very noses of the Turkish snipers. Luckily there were few casualties, and the seriousness of these was amply atoned for by the fresh meat we had for several days to come.

On the 24th it was again decided to shorten our line, and a new position was dug about a mile behind. That evening the 1-9th Gurkhas and 93rd evacuated the forward position, and retired to bivouacs behind the 59th Rifles, who occupied the new line.

Just about this time the activity of Fazal, as any Turkish airman was familiarly called, was very pronounced. They appeared to have complete mastery of the air. What a contrast to the days to come!

On the 28th, No. III D.C. under Captain Cummings, went to take up a river-picquet line north of Mason's Mounds, and during the same day the remainder of the regiment went to bivouacs on the banks of Thorny Nala.

It was obvious now that operations on a large scale would not be long delayed.

During the ensuing days we dug Twin Canal Redoubt, which was intended as a further stepping-off place after Sanna. Little did people think that seven months later this redoubt would be the most important railway station on the Sheikh Saad – Sinn railway. The operations were originally intended to start on 5 March, but were put off through threats of rain until 7 March. On the morning of the 7th, C.O.s and adjutants went to Brigade Headquarters for instructions. These orders were verbal; there were no written ones issued, and they included all orders up to the taking of first objectives.

The general idea was a holding attack on the east of Dujailah Redoubt, and a main attack on the same position from the south (Sketch No. 4). More detailed instructions were as follows. The 7th Brigade was to demonstrate east of Sinn Abtar Redoubt during 8 March, while on the same day, before dawn, the 36th, 28th, 9th, and 8th Brigades were to be in position in a semi-circular formation south of the Redoubt, in the order named, from west to east. The first three brigades were to attack the Redoubt, pass through, and take up a position along the edge of the Dujailah Depression to await the arrival of the Turkish reserves from Magasis. As soon as the Dujailah Redoubt was taken, the 8th Brigade was to advance on the Sinn Abtar Redoubt. After this, orders would be issued according to the existing situation. Meanwhile the cavalry was to sweep round in the direction of Imam al Mansur.

The position from which the 9th and 28th Brigades were to develop their attack was the two nalas running west from the elbow of the Dujailah Depression south of the Redoubt, and known as Kemball's Corner.

Of the Turks, only the following information was known. There was a large reserve at Magasis, and also a ferry close by, which could bring more men over from the left bank. As to how strongly the Sinn position itself was held, little information could be given.

The plan, on the face of it, was a bold one, and, with ordinary luck and skilful handling, was sure to succeed. We will see what happened.

Brigades paraded just before dusk on 7 March, and proceeded to the position of assembly, marked with lamps, near Twin Canal Redoubt. From here the formation of advance was each brigade in one line of half-battalions in fours. The interval between battalions was 20 yards, and between half-battalions 10 yards. All animals, except S.A.A. and tool mules, were brigaded.

The assembly of the different units took place without a hitch, but the march commenced late, and the column had not gone far when it was halted for a whole hour, the reason being loss of touch, and the late arrival of some artillery units. This halt cast a gloom over the proceedings, as it did not now appear possible to arrive in position before dawn, while the appearance of a crescent moon, with its attendant star, did not offer any consolation. Indeed, everyone expected the operations to be postponed until the next day.

The march was continued, however, without further interruption. This is probably one of the most memorable night marches ever undertaken by the British Army. Certainly no force of the strength that this was has advanced such a distance by night in an unbeaten enemy's country. The column exceeded 20,000 men, with attendant animals, transport, and guns, while the distance to the point of deployment was 18 miles. It took 12 hours to accomplish. The march was guided and paced by sappers, assisted in their bearings by a searchlight at Orah, and the periodic flash of signal guns from Townshend at Kut. A long night march under the best conditions is very trying, but it becomes doubly monotonous when the force engaged consists of the best part of two divisions in solid, square formation, and the pace in consequence rarely exceeds a mile an hour. When one is stepping smartly forward, physical exertion overcomes mental fatigue, but when one is slowly and mechanically placing one

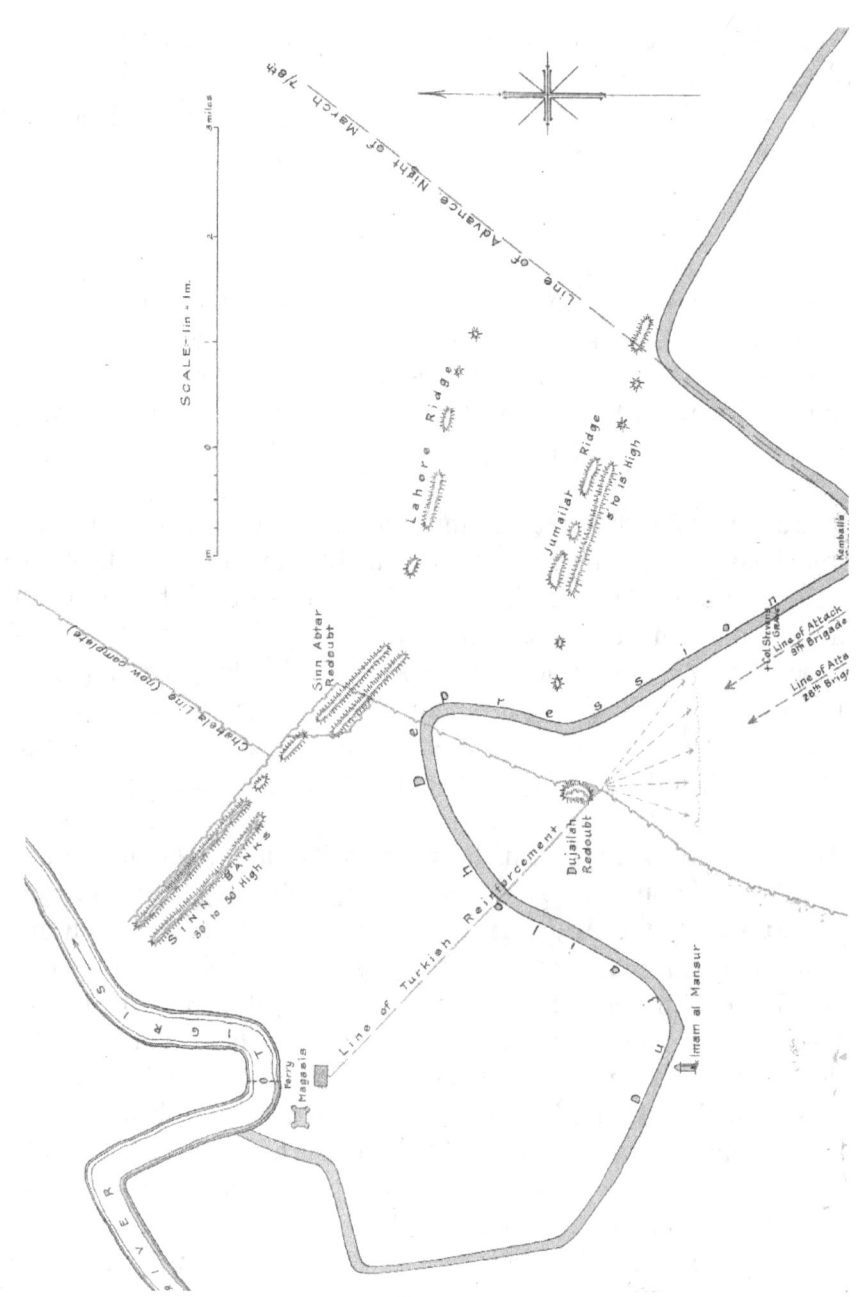

Sketch 4 The Battle of Dujailah. Chapter IV.

foot a few inches in front of the other, and doing it, moreover, for many hours at a stretch, there is no inducement for the brain to keep awake, until a trip or stumble brings one rudely back to life again. That night many men fell forward, and lay blissfully unconscious on the ground, until awakened by the impact of the foot of a man behind. For a smoker the desire for tobacco is almost irresistible, but of course stringent orders had been issued on that subject.

According to instructions the axles of all A.T. carts had been thoroughly greased. Their customary squeak was practically eliminated, but the rumble of their wheels, the shuffle of many thousand feet, the clang of equipment, and the occasional neigh of a frightened animal, made anyone in the column think that the noise it made could be heard for miles around. As a matter-of-fact, the harsher notes were lost in the general murmur of sound, and it is doubtful if anyone a few hundred yards away would have been conscious of our approach. The quality of sound resembled that of waves breaking on a far-off coast. That is to say, it would not catch the ear unless one especially listened for it. It is not a protracted volume of sound that draws the attention, but some single strident note.

After a fixed distance, pursuant to operation orders, formations were changed. Henceforth, the 1-1st Gurkhas advanced in one extended line, with the 93rd in one line of companies in fours behind. Next came the H.L.I. and 1-9th Gurkhas in one line of half-battalions. This unwieldy formation, combined with the fact that some empty Turkish trenches were met with, threw the column momentarily into indescribable confusion. Whole double-companies lost themselves, and it was some time before matters were re-adjusted.

During the weird half-light of early morning we could tell by the unevenness of the ground underfoot that we were entering the Depression. The column was still, we knew, some three miles from the position of deployment, where, had things gone according to plan, it should at that moment have been extended in its attack formations. On the flank, however, twinkled the fires of Arab encampments, so our presence was apparently a secret, and there still seemed to be a fair chance of success.

Through the haze of dawn loomed the vision of the Dujailah Redoubt, which had occupied our thoughts to the exclusion of all else, for some days past. It was a large oval-shaped mound some 80 feet high, such as commonly covers the remains of ancient cities in Mesopotamia.

Even from that distance it was obvious to the naked eye that it was honeycombed with trenches, which, however, appeared to be unoccupied. There were a few tents on the eastern slope, and from these a handful of men could be seen running for dear life. Had we gone straight for it we could probably have occupied the Redoubt without firing a shot. But we did not go straight for it. Firstly, the guns were called up to register, and so advertise our presence, then the 28th Brigade, which was behind, marched through while the 9th Brigade halted. When they had filed past, they, too, halted, and the 9th Brigade marched through them. Alas for these delays! How many brave lives were lost, how many subsequent valiant defeats were suffered, how many anxious eyes in Kut looked east in vain, because of them!

By 9 a.m. – three hours late – the brigade was in position, and the attack commenced. The leading battalions were the 1-1st Gurkhas, with their right on the Depression, and on their left the 93rd. The 1-9th Gurkhas were in support with half a battalion behind both the 1-1st Gurkhas and the 93rd. The H.L.I. were in reserve. The 28th Brigade attacked on the left of the 9th Brigade, while, to the right of the 9th, the 8th Brigade awaited the course of events so as to advance on Sinn Abtar.

The 93rd attacked in two waves, Nos I and III D.C.s, under Captain Morgan and Captain Cummings respectively, in front, and Nos II and IV D.C.s, under Major Simpson and Lieutenant Taylor, behind. As the attack commenced, line after line of grey-coated figures could be seen swarming over the Redoubt into the trenches (marked on Sketch No. 4 in dotted lines), the existence of which was previously unknown to us. These were the Turkish reserves from Magasis, whose time to reinforce coincided with our delays!

The reader must here again bear in mind the local topography of the country. To get to the concealed Turkish trench our attacking force had to advance over about two miles of ground. This was perfectly level, and without a vestige of cover. If the matter is given serious thought, it will become apparent that such an attack against a well-armed and disciplined enemy can only be successful under one of two conditions. These conditions are, firstly, that the attack should come as a surprise, i.e., under cover of darkness, so that the attackers are practically on the enemy before fire is opened, or, secondly, that the attackers be covered by such an intense gun and machine gun barrage that the enemy's morale is sufficiently shattered to render his fire innocuous.

Now, how did these conditions apply in this attack? Firstly, it had been intended as a surprise, but through delays had not gone according to plan, and was actually launched over three hours late. Secondly, the position of the dotted trench (Sketch No. 4) in which the enemy were sitting, was unknown to us, so that our guns were concentrated on the Redoubt itself, leaving a concealed enemy undisturbed, and able to scrape the ground with fire much as one would scrape mud off a boot with a penknife.

The attack was carried out with the utmost gallantry. Sikhs and P.M.s vied with each other in the rapidity of their advance, but the enemy's fire fell like hail, and men were falling fast. The leading lines had only advanced a hundred yards when they came under fire, and by the time some 2,000 yards had been covered the ground behind was a forest of rifles stuck in the ground, bayonet first, beside causalities. Our numbers had been so depleted that Major Simpson, who had now joined the front line, decided to halt and await reinforcements. So a friendly ditch some six inches deep was occupied, and consolidated. This ditch, it was afterwards discovered, was about four hundred yards from the concealed Turkish trench.

Meanwhile, Colonel Stevens, who was advancing with the last wave, was shot through the forehead, and died instantaneously, the command thereby devolving on Major Simpson.

To our left, the 28th Brigade (Leicesters, 51st and 53rd Sikhs, and 56th Rifles) drew level, and were also compelled to halt. The half-battalion of the 1-9th Gurkhas in support to the 93rd had also suffered badly, and very few got up to the front line.

Information was sent to Brigade Headquarters, which were in the nalas from where the attack started, and at 1 p.m. the H.L.I. advanced to our support. The intense fire, however, arrested them, and nothing came of it. During the afternoon the 8th Brigade attempted to take the Redoubt from the east, but their attack failed for the same reason as ours.

As dusk fell the fire slackened, and gradually ceased altogether, and instructions were received to dig in. The H.L.I. relieved the 1-1st Gurkhas on our right, and the 28th Brigade continued the line on our left. Besides Colonel Stevens, our casualties included Captain Morgan slightly wounded, Jemadars Mul Singh and Qadir Baksh killed, and Subadar Narain Singh, and Jemadars Mahbub Alam, Majhi Khan, and Indar Singh wounded. Our losses among officers, therefore, were comparatively light, but our total amounted to 190, or 45 percent. of the numbers engaged.

During the night we managed to bury all the dead, though, on revisiting the battlefield three months later, it was found that most of them had been dug up again. A padre very kindly came and read the burial service over Colonel Stevens' grave. The intensity of the fire may be gauged by the fact that when he was buried it was found that nine bullets had struck his body during the day.

The men were carrying two days' food in their haversacks, and Lieutenant Hobday, transport officer, sent up food for officers with commendable promptitude. Water of a slimy green colour was obtained from wells in the Depression, which was afterwards found to be full of corpses. However, most men's stomachs were tin-lined in those days.

So passed a sleepless night, during which our position was really a very precarious one. Our defence consisted in a continuous line of men occupying a slightly deepened water-cut. After the casualties of the day there were not sufficient men to keep supports behind, and the only reserve was a couple of weak regiments some 800 yards to the rear. Officers and men, moreover, were completely exhausted after the strain of the last 24 hours. The Turks, on the other hand, had only been on the move since dawn that day, and their casualties must have been infinitesimal. Had they made a determined attack that night there is little doubt that they would have thrown our force into the most indescribable confusion. Taking the initiative, however, was never the Turk's strong point, and mercifully we were left in comparative peace.

At midnight the enemy, who were evidently nervous, opened an intense burst of fire on us, and at the same time orders came to retire to the bend of the Depression from which the attack had developed. The failure of the attack, combined with a shortage of water, convinced the G.O.C. of the necessity of a general retirement. Accordingly, we removed the bolts and buried the rifles of all dead men, and, allowing the H.L.I. to get clear, closed in the Depression on the right at 3 a.m.

The retirement down the Depression was a gruesome affair. Dawn was just appearing, and the banks of the Depression were covered with line upon line of stretchers, and their suffering burdens. Lieutenant Pestonji and S.A.S. Lal Singh had worked all night, and had managed to get all our casualties transferred to I.F.A., but the difficulty was to get them back from there. There was not a single motor ambulance in Mesopotamia in early 1916, and the only means of transport back across the 23 miles or so of rough country to Camp C was by A.T. carts. The sufferings of the severely wounded by such means of transportation can be imagined. On some carts they were piled in two layers, and in this condition they jolted through the 10 weary and painful hours back to Camp C.

Arriving at the bend of the Depression, the 93rd took up a north-easterly direction from Kemball's Corner, to cover the evacuation of the wounded. The regiment stayed in this position until 12 noon, during which time the enemy kept up a continuous shell fire, but did little damage.

Orders came for the 9th and 28th Brigades to act as rearguard to the force when all was clear, and the 93rd and 51st Sikhs were detailed as the two brigades' respective rear-parties.

The retirement commenced soon after midday. The two regiments fell back side by side, and until Jumailat Ridges were passed, Nos. I and II D.C.s were kept fairly busy by Arab horsemen, who followed closely on their heels. For some reason, probably the thought of loot on the late battlefield, they soon gave up the chase, and afterwards the retirement was undisturbed. The remainder of the brigade paid very little attention to us, and, by the time we were clear of the enemy, only their dust was visible on the horizon.

The march back was a tedious affair. Reaction after the previous day's excitement had set in, and this, together with lack of sleep, produced a feeling of weariness and despondency among all ranks.

While passing Beit Aeissa the same battery that had given us trouble on 22 February again shelled the column, but with little effect.

Our original orders were to halt at Thorny Nala, where we arrived at 6 p.m., but to our sorrow, fresh instructions awaited us there to proceed to Camp C, another six miles further on. The regiment struggled into Camp C at 9 p.m. in a state of complete exhaustion. The men were too tired to eat the food which awaited them, though they had only had one meal in the last 48 hours. It is a comforting thought, however, that not a single man in the battalion fell out in the whole of the operations.

That General Campbell appreciated what the troops had done was evident from the message he sent around next day, which ran:-

> The O.C. Brigade wishes to place on record his appreciation and admiration of the gallantry displayed by all ranks of the brigade. It is estimated that in 51 hours, during two sleepless nights, the brigade marched 37 miles and fought a severe action, losing 730 of all ranks out of 2,350; this feat could only be accomplished by the greatest devotion to duty, gallantry, and efficiency.

To this there only remains to be added that not a single award was given to the regiment or brigade for their services. In these operations the Turk showed his great military weakness, i.e., lack of enterprise in taking the offensive. Had he counter-attacked during the night of 8/9 March, he would have converted an ordinary defeat into a hopeless rout; while the fact that he did not press more during the retirement shows bad generalship on his part. It was afterwards discovered that the troops who opposed us were, in the first instance, the 6th Infantry Regiment, afterwards reinforced by the famous 52nd Division, which had just arrived from Gallipoli.

Chapter V
Battle of Beit Aeissa, 17 April 1916

It is doubtful if these opening pages should be included in this chapter or the last. As they concern the retaking of the stepping-off place which enabled us to approach the enemy position of Beit Aeissa, they are included in this one.

The stepping-off place referred to is Abu Roman. Curious to relate, when our force retired from Dujailah, a garrison was kept at Twin Canal Redoubt, but Abu Roman and Mason's Mound were evacuated. The Turks promptly occupied them, and it was not until three weeks later that they again fell into our hands.

10 March, the day after the retirement from Dujailah, was a day of more or less peace, disturbed only by an enemy camel gun, which came up to the Umm al Brahm Marsh and shelled Camp C. A good night's rest, carried on late into the morning, had been very refreshing, but everyone still hoped for several days more undisturbed idleness. It came therefore as a rude shock when, during the evening of 10 March, orders came for the brigade to proceed at 4 a.m. next morning to Sanna.

Expecting to return in a few days' time, most of our kit was left behind. Actually the regiment never saw Camp C again, or the greater part of the kit they had left there.

The brigade arrived at Sanna just after daybreak, and it became evident that trouble was brewing towards Abu Roman, from which direction the unwelcome sound of intensive musketry was emanating. Orders came for the H.L.I. and 93rd to proceed to Abu Roman to support the 7th Brigade, which was engaged with the enemy.

During the march, many wounded were passed on their way to the dressing stations, and both regiments were halted in Thorny Nala, some two miles east of Abu Roman. Major Simpson and Colonel

Deacon of the H.L.I. were called to the 7th Brigade Headquarters for a conference. Meantime a heavy downpour had started, and everyone was soon drenched to the skin. The assembled C.O.s at Brigade Headquarters protested against the indefiniteness of the orders for the attack, and either because of this, or because of the rain, it was postponed, and we returned to Sanna, arriving there just before dusk.

The regiment bivouacked at Sanna until 13 March, when it moved to Twin Canal Redoubt, relieving there the 36th Sikhs, a regiment which had just arrived in the country. Two days later, the 1-9th Gurkhas relieved us at Twin Canals, and we moved to bivouacs about a mile north-east of the Redoubt, to a spot named Shand's Shanty.

Our rest did not last long. At midday next day Nos I and III D.C.s, under Captain Morgan, marched to Stack's Redoubt – a trench system recently dug out of Thorny Nala in the direction of Abu Roman (Sketch No. 5). In the evening of the same day, Battalion Headquarters and the remaining two double-companies joined them. On our left flank the H.L.I. occupied Highland Nala, while the 7th Brigade continued the line to the right. The day after our arrival at Stack's Redoubt Lieutenant Taylor went sick with colitis.

The situation at this time was very obscure. There was no regular trench system, and the Turkish line appeared to consist of picquets, and isolated snipers' posts. Though bullets flew in all directions, a Turk was never actually seen while we were in this position.

Orders were received to join up Stack's Redoubt with Highland Nala by a fire-trench, and at 2 a.m. on the 22nd, work commenced. While Lieutenant Bright was engaged in making a machine gun emplacement, a stray bullet hit him in the back, and he died a few minutes later. We buried him next morning halfway between Stack's Redoubt and the Lunette.

Bright's death was a great blow to the regiment. It was a case of absolute bad luck, his being the only casualty experienced that night. He was the fortunate possessor of a disposition which remained cheerful under the most adverse conditions. At the blackest times he could always conjure up a smile. He was very popular with the men, and his loss cast a gloom over the regiment for some time.

Next day, Lieutenant Drought rejoined. He had been very much delayed bringing the transport from France, but, unfortunately, was unable to bring officers' chargers with him.

At this period lice, of which nearly every officer and man had brought a stock with him from Burma Trenches, were at their worst. These vermin abound in Mesopotamia when the ground is damp, and as everyone always slept on the ground, and considered themselves lucky with one bath a month, there was no difficulty in collecting them. Otherwise perfectly well-mannered field officers, while at mess waiting for their bully and onions, might be seen sitting with ecstatic face and hard at work beneath their shirt fronts. As soon as the hot weather came, and we changed into thin clothing, they disappeared.

On 24 March, the regiment was relieved in Stack's Redoubt by the H.L.I., and retired to bivouacs a short way east of Thorny Nala. The next few days were spent in building bunds along the edge of Thorny Nala to keep out the river flood, which was daily expected.

On the 29th, according to orders, the regiment marched back to Burma Trenches and Arab Village, Nos I and IV D.C.s going to the latter, and Battalion Headquarters, with Nos II and III D.C.s to the former. Although the various companies came under considerable fire from the other bank while getting into position, no casualties were suffered.

The 13th Division, which had just arrived from Gallipoli, was at this time concentrating behind the 7th Division at Hannah. It was evident, from the amount of registering and other preparations that took place, that a second attempt to take Hannah was contemplated, and everyone thought that the regiment would be employed in its former role of supplying enfilade fire from Burma Trenches. This, however, was not destined to be done by us, as the 93rd were relieved next day by the 62nd Punjabis, and marched back to Sanna, where the whole 3rd Division was gradually concentrating.

While at Sanna, two changes took place in the regiment. On 1 April, Lieutenant Pestonji was replaced by one Sen Gupta, a Bengali. Everyone was very sorry to lose Pestonji. He had been with the battalion about nine months, and during that time had again and again shown his sterling qualities. During the attack on 21 January, though very ill, he had refused to go sick, and on 8 March, through sheer hard work, had managed to evacuate our wounded before those of any other regiment in the brigade. This, combined with the pleasantest of dispositions, had endeared him to everyone in the regiment. The day following Pestonji's departure, Major Haughton, from the 92nd Punjabis, joined as permanent second in command, and to command the regiment until the arrival of Colonel Whitehead, who, it will be remembered, had gone to Gallipoli, and had now been ordered to rejoin. Major Simpson in consequence returned to No. II D.C.

Lieutenant Wilsey, of the 72nd Punjabis, also joined at this time as a reinforcement.

Orders were now received for the second Battle of Hannah. The 13th Division was to attack at 5 a.m. on 5 April, and the 3rd Division was to be ready to advance on the right bank according to the progress made on the left.

After an intense bombardment the 13th Division attacked and carried the Hannah position, which had been almost deserted by the Turks, and advanced on round the bend. Their progress could be followed from Sanna by watching the monitors, which steamed up close behind.

At 9.30 a.m. the 9th Brigade received orders to advance. The enemy abandoned Abu Roman in front of the 3rd Division, and fell back on their now completed trenches at Beit Aeissa.

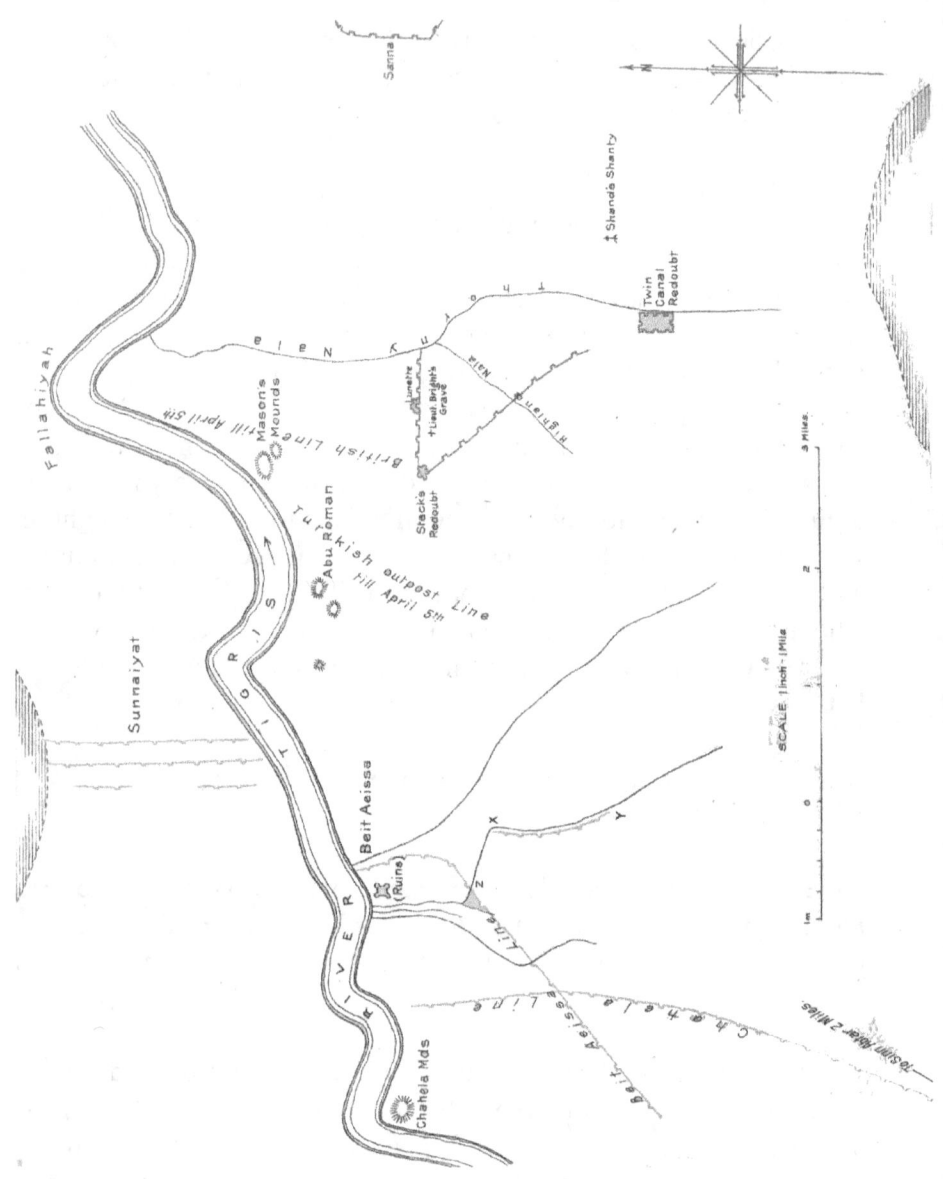

Sketch 5. Sanna-Beit Aeissa. Chapter V

That night, the brigade took up an outpost position, of which the 93rd formed the left flank at Twin Canal Redoubt. Meanwhile the 13th Division had followed up the Turk, and had stormed the enemy's line at Fallahtyah. The capture of these two positions on the left bank was really not so important as it at first appeared. The Turks had not expected to hold us up at either, but were only fighting delaying actions before we came up against their main position at Sunnaiyat. This position at Sunnaiyat was extremely strong, lying, like Hannah, with its right on the river and its left on the marsh. During the ensuing 10 days two costly attempts were made to break through at Sunnaiyat, both of which failed.

On 11 April, the brigade was ordered to concentrate about three miles west of Twin Canals. In order to do this, and avoid the floods, it had to march to Abu Roman, cross the flood by a causeway a few feet wide, and turn south through a sea of mud. That night was spent in one of the most miserable bivouacs it has been our lot to experience. It poured steadily all night, and while lying in six inches of mud and water, sleep eludes all but the weariest.

On the night of 12 April, we marched up to the point which had been our headquarters on 22 February, to support the 8th Brigade, but returned the next day.

It is here necessary to explain the differences between Sketches No. 5 and No. 6. It will be noticed that they do not tally either in regard to the various nalas, or in regard to the enemy's trenches. The reason for this is that Sketch No. 5 is a copy of the map issued before the operations, and No. 6 is a copy of that issued afterwards, when the whole of the ground was in our hands, and had been properly surveyed. The latter is the more accurate, and should be referred to in the following narrative.

At this time the main Turkish line on the right bank in front of Sinn was at Beit Aeissa, but they occupied, and had traversed, the nala X-

Y running roughly north and south some half-mile east of it. The 7th and 8th Brigades were engaged in driving in any picquets that the enemy held in front of this.

It was now obvious that the next move was to be made on the right bank, and at 8 p.m. on the 13th, C.O.s and adjutants went to Brigade Headquarters to hear details of the preliminary operations, which were to commence at midnight that day. There was an absolute deluge on at the time, and, much to everyone's relief, after the scheme had been explained, a divisional wire came cancelling it. Soon after, the rain stopped, and the ground dried sufficiently to enable the operations to be proceeded with.

On the night of 14 April, the brigade marched out to the position from where the attack on the traversed nala mentioned above was to commence at dawn next day.

The 27th Punjabis occupied a picquet line some 300 yards in front of this nala, and the 93rd were detailed to relieve them (Sketch No. 6). This was accomplished by midnight. The 7th and 9th Brigades were to attack at dawn, and capture the nala, as no operations against the main position at Beit Aeissa could take place while this nala remained in Turkish hands.

The two brigades advanced through the 93rd picquets, and captured the nala with little opposition, as the attack came as a complete surprise. Three men of No. III D.C. earned the I.D.S.M. this day for conspicuous gallantry in bringing in the wounded.

Fairly intense fire was kept up all day by enemy concealed in the long grass between the nala and the Beit Aeissa trenches, and that night the 93rd again relieved the 27th Punjabis in the nala, the 7th Brigade on relief being withdrawn to the north. Our sentries suffered rather heavily that night through enemy snipers, who crawled up quite close to our line through the long vegetation.

We were now up against the main position of Beit Aeissa, the importance of which lay in the three nalas behind, by means of which the enemy could flood the low-lying land in front of Sinn Banks at will. If another move was to be made against the Sinn position, Beit Aeissa would have to be captured first, as an encircling movement would otherwise always court the disaster of having the line of retreat cut off by inundations.

It was decided to attack Beit Aeissa on 17 April. On the afternoon of the 16th, C.O.s and adjutants went to meet General Campbell at the point X (Sketch No. 6), where the scheme was explained. The 8th Brigade were to relieve the 9th Brigade in the nala X-Y that evening. The attack would be carried out by the 7th and 9th Brigades from right to left respectively, the right of the 7th Brigade resting on the river, and the left of the 9th Brigade on the point X mentioned above.

After relief the brigade was to close to the right and dig itself in in four lines, the left of the front line (1-1st Gurkhas) on point X, and the frontage 600 yards north-east. The other three lines were to be 25 yards behind each other, and were to be dug and occupied by the 1-9th Gurkhas, 93rd, and H.L.I. respectively. Brigade Headquarters was to be at the Twin Pimples, two high mud O.P.s.

Each regiment was thus in one line. As soon as the 1-1st Gurkhas advanced, the 1-9th Gurkhas were to occupy the line they evacuated, and similarly the 93rd would occupy the line evacuated by the 1-9th Gurkhas. Thus as each regiment advanced, those behind moved up one place. The H.L.I. were, however, not to take part in the attack, but were to remain in reserve. Operation Orders stated that they were only to be used in case of dire necessity. The reason for this was not obvious at the time, as little did we think they intended to use the 3rd Division again next day to take Sinn Abtar.

The idea of a regiment advancing to the attack in one line may seem queer nowadays, but it must be remembered that the strength of the 93rd in this attack was only 300 rifles. As soon as it had been relieved that evening by the 59th Rifles, the regiment closed on the right, and dug in successfully.

Everyone had expected to be punished rather severely while digging in. There was a full moon, and fate had sent a cloudless night, apparently to increase our discomfiture. The enemy line was only 800 yards away, and they had a bombing block and picquet several hundred yards in front of this up the nala X-Z. Strange to relate, however, very little firing took place, in fact, our only casualty that night was Jemadar Sher Khan, who was shot through the leg.

The lines that were dug were not a continuous trench, but a series of funk pits to give the occupants protection while asleep. The work was complete by 1 a.m. and the brigade composed themselves for slumber in the holes they had dug. Little rest, however, came that night, except for the fitful and uneasy sleep which always precedes an attack the following day.

Slowly dawn broke on a grey and murky day – a day which was, perhaps, the most eventful in the history of the regiment. The advance, preceded by a 25-minute bombardment, was not timed to take place until 6.45 a.m. This left over an hour of daylight, during which everyone had to lie full length in their respective holes. Had a soul stirred out of them it might have given the whole plan away to the enemy, as they knew that previously our line had not extended north of the point X. It was a miserable hour. One yearned for hot tea and a cigarette, but even the smoke of the latter might have let the cat out of the bag. One could only lie, and twiddle one's thumbs, and wonder where one would be in a few hours' time. There is, nevertheless, something very thrilling in waiting for the opening of one's own bombardment. Watches have been synchronised, and everyone lies waiting, and pitying the poor devils in the burrow opposite. At a second before time a whistling is heard in the air, growing louder and louder, for all the world like a flock of starlings. It passes overhead, and one instinctively looks up as if to see the shells, little ones, big ones, and thumping great heavies, sail by. There is a deafening crash, and lo! Hell is let loose on earth.

This bombardment was the largest we had yet seen in Mesopotamia, and the Turkish trenches were soon lost in a cloud of white, black, and yellow smoke. At 6.45 a.m. the 1-1st Gurkhas advanced, and the 1-9th Gurkhas and 93rd each moved up one place. Soon after, the 1-9th Gurkhas advanced, and our battalion occupied the old 1-1st Gurkha line. Our turn soon came. Although we passed through heavy enfilade machine gun fire from the left, that is to say, from that part of the Turkish line not bombarded, very few casualties were suffered during the advance. Indeed, the smoke was so dense that the advancing lines must have offered a very poor target.

As soon as the regiment arrived in the Turkish front line, No. 1 D.C., under Lieutenant Trevelyan, went forward to reinforce the 1-1st Gurkhas, who were in the enemy's second line in the nalas in front. The remainder of the battalion, led by No. III D.C. and the left wing bombers, moved southwards down the old Turkish trench in the direction of A5 – A6. This trench, especially along the narrow passages behind traverses, was choc-a-block with Turkish dead and dying. In some places they lay four and five deep, mangled by the most atrocious shell wounds. They had to be thrown out on to the parados to allow us a passage. Except, perhaps, in the Mahomed Abdul Hassan Bend, we never encountered so many Turkish dead in one day.

The trenches up to the line A6 – A8 (Sketch No. 6) were soon cleared of the enemy, and the 93rd occupied the line from A7 through A8 to A6, with No. II D.C. in support with Battalion Headquarters in the shallow nala at A5. On our right were the 1-9th Gurkhas, then the 1-1st Gurkhas, and finally the 7th Brigade up to the river bank. Just on our right front the 1-9th Gurkhas captured two field guns. These were the cause of a lot of trouble, and will be referred to again.

The remnants of the enemy had fled across country in a south-westerly direction towards Sinn Abtar, and kept up a fairly accurate rifle fire from various nalas en route. Our shrapnel found them out wherever they collected, however, for when this ground was seen by us some months later, it was found that every little nala contained its quota of corpses. At midday all fire ceased.

Up to the present, we had only suffered 13 casualties in the attack. The men's minds had been inflamed both by tales of, and the sight of, mutilated bodies of our men, and certain excesses took place, which will not be described, as they might leave a false impression in the mind of a reader not in possession of all the facts of the case.

In order to understand the calamity which was shortly to befall us, two points must be borne in mind, neither of which redounds to the credit of anyone in the brigade.

Firstly, everyone was so pleased with the result of the attack, that little or no effort was made at consolidation, and our left at the point A6 remained a salient, instead of being joined up with the 8th Brigade, who were still in the nala X-Y echeloned some 2,000 yards to the left rear.

Secondly, information was received that a brigade of the 13th Division would relieve us at Beit Aeissa that evening, and that the 3rd Division would push on to attack Sinn Abtar next day. These orders arrived at midday, and, as a result, our reserve S.A.A., which had been ordered up, was stopped, and the only ammunition left was that in our pouches and bandoliers, which itself was by now somewhat depleted.

At 5 p.m. British officers were collected at Battalion Headquarters at A5, and were engaged in cooking sausages. Simultaneously the Turks started a mild barrage, but as the shells passed well overhead little attention was paid to it. Suddenly a report came on the telephone that masses of Turks were advancing from the direction of Sinn Abtar.

It is not contended that the ensuing tale is correct in every detail. It is really only an account of personal impressions, which, especially as the action was fought by night, are bound to be very localised. Those who have seen war from a regimental officer's point of view know that the memories of an action retained in the mind are as those of a dream – hazy or clear according to the bitterness or otherwise of the fight. Events of trivial importance sometimes remain impressed on the mind, while those many times more vital slip the memory.

Many people, however, are certain that the two guns captured by the 1-9th Gurkhas, and the company which was guarding them, were the commencement of our undoing.

As soon as the enemy were within range, our fire opened. The ideal thing, of course, would have been to have withheld fire until they were quite close, but the Turks had timed their attack to such a nicety that this was impossible. Night was falling fast, and soon all targets would have become obscured in the dusk.

While it lasted, our fire must have been of extraordinary intensity, but ammunition was limited, and before long it gave out. Not a round was left in the regiment. The machine gun section even filled their belts from the rounds in their bandoliers. By this time the Turks were within a few yards of the brigade, which broke, beginning with the point to which the 1-98th Gurkha company had retired to from the guns. The Gurkha's fire at this place had, of course, been masked while the company was in front, and the Turkish advance was unhindered. Once the line on our right had broken, it would have been suicidal to stay, as we were momentarily expecting to have our left enveloped, this flank being a complete salient, with a gap of about 2,000 yards between us and the 8th Brigade.[3] Once the retirement started it was one of complete disorder.

It was a never to be forgotten sight, and the pale moonlight, the zip-zip of the bullets, and the dismal war cry of the Turks added to the eeriness of it. It resembled nothing so much as a crowd breaking up, and streaking for the gates after a football match. It was impossible to reform. British, Indians, Gurkhas, and Turks, were all mixed up, and the lack of cohesion occasioned by this destroyed all morale. If a line of 20 men was collected, it as like as not included a few enemy,

---

[3] Edmund Candler in *Long Road to Baghdad* (Boston & New York: Houghton Mifflin, 1919) is wrong in saying this point was held by the Gurkhas. It was held by the 93rd.

and at the best the flanks always dribbled away until nothing was left.

While moving along, one often found that the man next door was a Turk, equally unaware of the identity of his neighbour.

By this time our guns had wind of the affair, though they did not know how far our line had retired. It was a question of trusting to luck, and they put down a barrage halfway between the two lines. This, unfortunately, was the identical spot where we were, and, though it had the advantage of arresting the Turkish element, our men had to pass through it, and suffered accordingly. We had now arrived at the Twin Pimples, and with great difficulty a line was formed in the original trench from which the 1-1st Gurkhas had attacked. This, having been constructed in an existing nala, was the only one of the lines which gave continuous cover. While the line was being re-formed, Major Simpson was shot through the head. He lived sufficiently long to call for the adjutant, but was unconscious when he arrived, and died soon afterwards.

About the same time, Major Haughton received a severe bomb wound in the thigh, and, while he was being helped along, a bullet wound through the chest. Subadar Gurmukh Singh was also killed, Jemadar Partab Singh wounded, and Lieutenant Haycraft slightly wounded in the head.

There was no news of either Captain Morgan or Lieutenant Wilsey, so that only Captain Cummings and Lieutenants Drought, Haycraft, and Trevelyan were left with the regiment.

Luckily ammunition was found in the trench, and a busy time was spent reorganising, the necessary respite being caused by our barrage, which made the enemy swerve to their right, and so come up against the hitherto untouched 8th Brigade. The Turks, having lost their sense of direction, must now have been completely demoralised. The fire of the 8th Brigade, which continued in bursts all night, completed their discomfiture, and the counter-attack died a natural death. The brigade of the 13th Division, which was to have relieved us, arrived, and filled the gap between the 9th and 8th Brigades, and no further organised attack was made on our front, though it was a night of horrible suspense. They made repeated efforts to bomb up the nala to the point X, where our left rested. All night this nala was the scene of an intense bombing duel, with varying fortunes to both sides. Many Turks were killed at the point X itself, but by dawn our bombers had driven them back some hundreds of yards down the nala.

18 April broke a clear and sultry day. With the first appearance of light, bodies of Turks rose from the grass close to our front, and fled back to the original Turkish line, which they had recaptured the night before. While watching these, Lieutenant Drought was struck in the face by the splinters of a bayonet, which protruded above the trench, and which was shivered by an enemy bullet. At the time, the wound looked very severe, and he was removed to the dressing-station.

Very welcome news arrived that Captain Morgan and Lieutenant Wilsey were both alive and well, though Lieutenant Wilsey had been slightly wounded. They had both got separated in the retirement with bodies of men, and had edged off further to the left.

During the whole of that morning, and well on in the afternoon, the brigade was packed in the narrow nala. It was very hot, and there was no room to move, and scarcely air enough to breathe. It was impossible to move from one point in the trench to another, without getting outside, and this meant certain death from the enemy machine gun posts, now established within a few hundred yards of our line. A number of men, who were forced to leave the trench in this way, were lost during the day. During the afternoon we were relieved, and retired in small parties to bivouacs some two miles south-east of the point X. Here the roll was called, and of the 300 who had gone into action, 154 answered their names. In other words, our casualties had been practically 50 percent; but, added to this, we had suffered an absolutely irreparable loss in the death of Major Simpson. For 20 years his had been the leading spirit of the regiment. Beloved alike by officers and men, who would have followed him to the end of the world, he was a perfect type of that perfect man – an English gentleman. Let those that follow in the regiment read these, and not think them empty, words. The name of Major Simpson should be revered by us as embodying all that is best in the regimental spirit and traditions.

The loss of Subadar Gurmukh Singh was also a great blow. Though a Sikh of the new school, with very advanced ideas, his mind was exceedingly straight, and free from bias.

We heard that day that Major Haughton had arrived at the Field Ambulance safely, and though very severely wounded, was doing well.

That evening Captain Barrett, who, it will be remembered, had been wounded on 21 January, rejoined, and took over No. II D.C.

Next day we were visited by General Campbell, who was most enthusiastic in his praise of the regiment, and its steadiness in being the first to reform. With the General came Mr Candler, the official correspondent, to hear the tale of Subadar Major Mahomed Baksh, who, having lost his revolver, downed and strangled an enormous Turk. Unfortunately, in his account of the incident, Mr Candler referred to the Subadar Major as "a magnificent bearded Sikh."

The doings of S.A.S. Lal Singh are also worthy of record. During the retirement our medical officer did not stay at his post, and Lal Singh evacuated his entire hospital under the severest fire, also finding time to rescue a stranded machine gun, which would otherwise have fallen into the hands of the Turks.

News afterwards came that the troops which counter-attacked that night were the 2nd Division, of fame in Gallipoli and the Balkan War, and generally considered one of the finest divisions of the Turkish Army. They were supported by the 35th Division, and left 3,000 dead in front of our trenches. The Turkish G.O.C. afterwards admitted having 10,000 casualties that night.

The Battle of Beit Aeissa,[4] in the way of casualties, was the biggest action fought by the Kut Relief Force. More Turks were killed than in any three other battles together, and two enemy divisions were put altogether out of action.

We met the 2nd Turkish Division again, to our cost, just a year later at the Jebel Hamrin.

---

[4] The biggest action as regards numbers engaged was the Battle of Dujailah

Chapter VI
Battle of The Apex – 24 April 1916

After the casualties at Beit Aeissa, the fighting strength of the regiment, augmented by a few returned casualties, only amounted to about 160 rifles. This made the double-company organisation farcical, and hereafter the battalion was divided into two units – one of P.M.s and one of Sikhs, the latter being very much in the majority.

We were not left long in rest. On 21 April, the 93rd relieved the Manchesters in some new trenches east of the Triangle (Sketch No. 6), and the same evening the 2nd Rajputs in the Triangle itself.

While here, Lieutenant Drought rejoined, his wound not having proved as serious as it had at first appeared.

A third, and equally unsuccessful, attempt was made on Sunnaiyat on 22 April. The failure of this attack actually destroyed any hope there was of relieving Kut, as it reduced the 7th Division to a condition like that of the 3rd Division, i.e., one which rendered any further serious operations impossible.

Next day, orders were received to send an officer's patrol to proceed as far down Brigade Nala as possible, and reconnoitre the Apex and Sugarloaf (Sketch No. 6).

Patrolling by day in Mesopotamia is a most difficult proceeding. Distances are almost impossible to judge across the featureless desert, and if the sun is shining, the horizon is soon lost in a hazy mirage, through which objects contort themselves into the most fantastic shapes. A man becomes a telegraph pole, a horse an elongated camel, while a clump of bushes might be anything from a forest to a thickly populated village. This patrol, then, under Lieutenant Wilsey was unable to discover much; but the fact of its dispatch sounded ominous, and proved to be so.

After dark, the C.O. (Captain Morgan) and adjutant were called to

Brigade Headquarters, to hear the not very welcome news that the brigade would make an attack at dawn next day, 24 April. The object of the operation was the capture of the Apex, an isolated enemy trench system covering the southern flank of Beit Aeissa.

The brigade would rendezvous at the Triangle at 3 a.m. From here it would march in the order 93rd, H.L.I., 1-1st Gurkhas, 1-9th Gurkhas, to a selected point down the nala known as Brigade Nala, from where the attack would commence.

On arrival at this point in the nala, the 93rd and H.L.I. were to right turn, quit the nala, and lie down about 10 yards outside. Meanwhile the 1-1st Gurkhas and 1-9th Gurkhas were to file down until they covered the former two regiments, and also right turn. The brigade would then be in two lines, the 93rd and H.L.I. forming the front line, and the 1-1st and 1-9th Gurkhas the second lime. In order to understand this extraordinary formation for attack it must be remembered that no unit exceeded 200 rifles. The advance would commence just before dawn, C.O.s were to keep on the inner flanks of their battalions, and the bearing of the advance was 230 degrees. It was not known quite how far the Apex was from Brigade Nala, and our instructions were to advance on no account more than 1,200 yards. These latter orders must be borne in mind to understand the predicament in which the regiment later found itself. Being very strong in British officers compared with other ranks, both Captain Cummings and Lieutenant Trevelyan were left behind.

Everything worked smoothly up to the time that the attack opened. The brigade reached the point in the nala, and formed up into two lines, but there was an unaccountable delay in getting the order to advance. Only a short time was wanting before dawn, and the whole success of the operation seemed likely to be imperilled. Luckily, the inability of the 93rd to pass a verbal order correctly saved the situation. The order was passed down to Captain Barrett, who was at the other end of the line, to "be ready to advance." By the time the message reached him, the first three words had been omitted, and to the astonishment of Brigade Headquarters, the 93rd suddenly

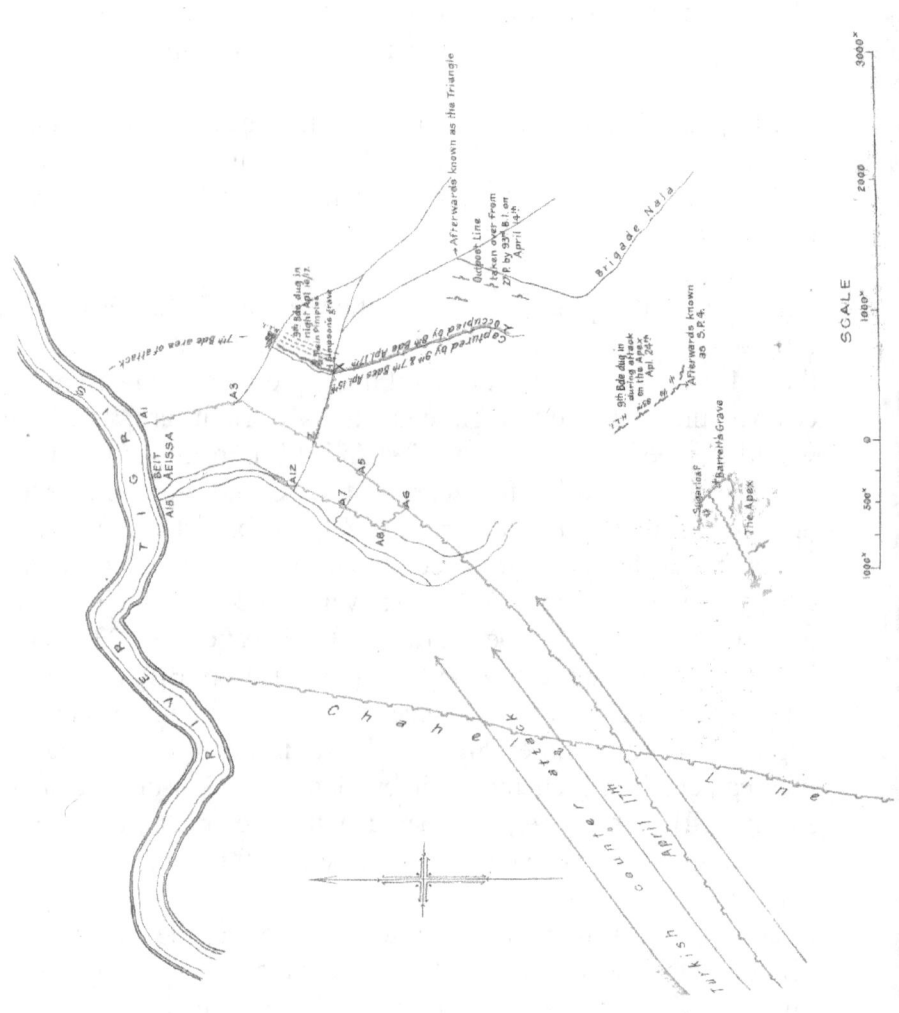

Sketch 6 The Battles of Beit Aeissa and Apex. Chapters V and VI

disappeared into the blue, the H.L.I. following suit.

It was a beautiful morning. The first tints of dawn crowned the rugged Pusht-i-Kuh, and the larks sang merrily overhead in the still air as if in all the world there was no such thing as war; but we were rudely awakened. The enemy had pushed out picquets well in front of their position, and these, after a few minutes' rapid fire to warn their comrades, retired. The men behaved splendidly. After the first quiver down the ranks when fire was opened, they advanced as steadily as if on parade. This cold, calculating advance at dawn, when the offensive spirit is at its lowest, against an enemy who fires from unexpected quarters, and without the music of a single friendly gun, is perhaps the greatest test men can be put to. The advance continued through the half-light of early morning, and the increasing enemy fire appeared to come from all directions, including the one we had come from.

At last day broke, and to everyone's consternation the Apex and Sugarloaf (a large O.P.) could be seen, still some 800 yards away. The brigade signallers informed Captain Morgan that they had already laid out 1,500 yards of wire, and the orders were to advance on no account more than 1,200 yards!

Our advancing lines were now under observation from the Apex, and a perfect hail of bullets commenced to fall. After a hasty consultation with Captain Gerrard, who commanded the H.L.I., Captain Morgan decided to halt, and consolidate in a friendly nala close by. This nala was only six inches deep, and while digging in, Subadar Major Mahomed Baksh was hit through the head. He bled profusely. Three bandages would not stop the flow, and, as the grand old man was being carried away, he cried out, "Never mind, Sahib, I'll be back soon." Poor Mahomed Baksh! He died at Amara some three weeks later, too early to hear of the I.O.M. he had so deservedly earned. He was undoubtedly the most gallant Indian Officer that ever served in the battalion.

Lieutenant Drought was also shot through the shoulder, and had to return to the dressing-station. He never rejoined the regiment during the war. Our thanks are due to him for the state of proficiency to which he brought our machine gun section.

It soon became evident that the Turks were evacuating the Apex. Two guns were successfully limbered up, and got away, while bodies of men retired under the fire of others. Patrols, pushed out soon after, reported the Apex to be empty.

At this time some Turkish cavalry and guns got round our left flank, and began to shell us rather heavily in enfilade, and the only instructions obtainable from brigade were to send a strong patrol forward to occupy the Apex. Accordingly, 25 men of No. II D.C. under Captain Barrett set out, and had not gone far when a message came from Brigade Headquarters cancelling the order. A runner was sent to recall them, but they returned, alas, without their leader. While Captain Barrett was standing on the edge of the Apex, he caught the full burst of a H.E. shell. He was horribly mangled, but mercifully his end must have been painless. Poor "Boo," as he was commonly called! Better known at the bars, and racecourses of Burma, than in more refined society, he combined the cheeriest of dispositions with the best of natures, and, as such, was a dreadful loss to a regiment on service.

Not long afterwards our cavalry dealt with the Turks on the left flank, and so the action closed. Our losses in this attack were 40. This may seem small enough, but nevertheless it was 29 percent of our strength. Besides Lieutenant Drought and Subadar Major Mahomed Baksh, Subadar Harnam Singh and Jemadars Taihal Singh, Ghazan Khan, and Mahomed Dim were wounded.

The corner on our left, where the Gurkhas had come up and refused the flank in order to meet the threat of the enemy cavalry, was afterwards known as S.P.4, and will be referred to again.

The regiment remained in this line until 29 April, when it was relieved by the 26th Punjabis. A few days before the relief, Captain

Cummings complained of feeling unwell, and later became so bad that he had to be transferred to the ambulance. To our horror, next morning news arrived that he had died during the night of cholera. Having come through all the fighting unscathed, it was appalling luck to be taken away when it was all finished.

The presence of cholera did not tend to raise our already depressed spirits, and the death of Captain Gerrard, O.C., H.L.I., made matters look rather serious. However, except for one other death, there were no more cases in the regiment.

It was now obvious that the relief of Kut was impossible, and it came as no surprise to learn that General Townshend had capitulated on 29 April.

Thus closed the operations of the Kut Relief Force, our share having reduced the regiment from a fighting strength of 735 to 96, and its morale from one of intense keenness to one of gloomy depression.

Our casualties in the Kut Relief operations amounted to over 400 killed and wounded. Considering the many actions in which the regiment was engaged, this may not appear to be a large number; but it must be remembered that, besides the 735 men that had been brought into the country, only eight men were received as reinforcements, and as each successive attack took place, the regiment went in with steadily decreasing numbers. Thus in the last attack we had only about 160 men engaged. Had the regiment been filled up with new drafts after each attack, as happens in most campaigns, the casualties would have been very much higher.

The only criterion in estimating casualties is their percentage to the numbers engaged. Including all employed, and other non-effective men, our percentages in this campaign were, British officers 86 percent, other ranks 56 percent. If the former (i.e. non-effectives) are excluded, the percentages amount to 100 percent and 70 percent respectively.

Chapter VII
Hot Weather, 1916

After relief by the 26th Punjabis, the regiment marched back to camp about a mile behind Brigade Nala. Here we lived in tents for the first time since leaving Camp C on 11 March.

While in this Camp the brigade was inspected by General Lake, the G.O.C. Great was the consternation in higher circles when they found that the battalion frontage of the 93rd in quarter-column was six yards!

The morale of the regiment in May 1916 was lower, as is natural, than at any other period of the war. Apart from the fact of casualties, among them one's best friends, there was the horrible feeling that there was nothing to show for it, and that the whole campaign would have to be fought again to bring the Turk to his knees.

The discomforts, too, were many. It was getting intensely hot – the thermometer registering 115 degrees – and there was no covering except 40lb tents. The flies were worse than anything imaginable – with many thousands of decaying corpses lying unburied around Beit Aissa it is no wonder. There is no exaggeration in saying that when the flies were disturbed, the opposite end of the mess tent was hidden by the cloud, and that when they settled on the tent roof at night, it appeared as a black ceiling above one's head. A fairly large percentage in bulk of the food which passed one's lips was flies. It was absolutely impossible to keep them out, and if the food was sweet it made matters doubly worse. Jam had to be discarded as an article of diet altogether. How different it was in after years, with E.P. tents for officers, and canteens almost at one's door! In 1916 it was a 40lb tent on a blank, blazing plain, sometimes six to eight miles from the river, and with just enough water to drink, and little to wash in. It was porridge and 'herrings-in'[5] for breakfast, bully and rice for tiffin, and bully and onions for dinner. Bully eaten occasionally makes quite an

---

[5] Herrings in tomato sauce. (ed.)

agreeable meal; but in the hot weather one's stomach rebels against it, when it slips out of the tin a slimy red mass, and, moreover, is served every day for about six months. How one longed for a fresh joint with potatoes and green vegetables!

Among the many other plagues and pests of Mesopotamian hot weather, is the dust-devil. With a wet towel around his head, the occupant of a 40lb tent lies stripped to the waist, vainly trying to pass the unbearable hours until sunset in sleep and forgetfulness. There is a sudden swirl, and clothes, papers, everything, leaps to a mad dance in a whirl of dust. It passes, but leaves behind a grimy body, from which the dust runs off in rivulets of sweat, the whole enveloped in a blue haze of blasphemy.

On 8 May, the regiment again moved into the front line near S.P.4, and while there the awards for the Battle of Beit Aeissa were published, and the ribbons were presented by General Keary at a parade of the 7th and 9th Brigades. Our share included three I.O.M. for Subadar Major Mahomed Baksh, Subadar Indar Singh, and S.A.S. Lal Singh, and three I.D.S.M.s. These, with the I.D.S.M. gained on 21 January, and a Military Cross published later, were the only decorations received by the regiment for the whole campaign. They would have been an ordinary allotment for one action later in the war.

At the medal-presentation parade there were no new ribbons available, and a few had to be hastily gathered from people already in possession of them. Even then there were not enough to go round, and the farcical ceremony was gone through of presenting one man with a ribbon, and then taking it back to give to another.

During this period the brigade staff underwent considerable change. Captain Buckland, D.S.O., 8th Gurkhas, relieved Captain Hamilton, M.C., as brigade major, and Captain Crawford, 89th Punjabis, took over staff captain from Captain Reinhold. Captain Crawford did not keep the appointment long, handing it over to Captain Bostock, Manchester Regiment, in August.

The line from Beit Aeissa through S.P.4. would have been our hot weather line for 1916 had the Turks not ultimately retired, and our time was spent in digging the elaborate network of trench systems, which were very soon afterwards abandoned.

On the morning of 19 May, the 9th Brigade was relieved by the 8th Brigade, and marched back to rest. We had no sooner arrived there than news came that the Turks had evacuated Beit Aeissa, and were falling back on Sinn. Simultaneously orders came for the 3rd Division to concentrate by night near S.P.4. Accordingly, we packed up again, and marched at 6 p.m. On the way, Lieutenant Trevelyan, who had been sick a few days with jaundice, rejoined the regiment, also Lieutenant Wilsey, who had just gone through a machine gun course, and henceforth commanded the section.

Our chargers also arrived for this march – the first time we had seen them since leaving France. Lack of horses had greatly added to the discomforts of officers in the previous campaign, as, apart from riding them, they can carry all kinds of things, in addition to the authorised kit.

The 3rd Division bivouacked that night just outside S.P.4, and operation orders were received at 3.30 a.m. next morning. The 9th Brigade was to march straight for Dujailah Redoubt, the garrison of which might be there to receive them, or might not. The march was to be in diamond formation, of which the 93rd would be right flank battalion.

It was half expected that a second Battle of Dujailah would take place, since, although the Turks had evacuated Beit Aeissa, few people thought they would leave the Sinn position as well.

As soon as day broke it became intensely hot, and the march was very trying. Water soon gave out, and relays of motor lorries, which had now arrived in Mesopotamia for the first time, were unable to cope with the demand. People were surprised at the time that the motors were able to carry on across the rough country. They would have been greatly astonished had they been able to visualise the convoys of Ford vans, sometimes covering 10 miles of country, which accompanied the army in the campaign of the following year.

This time Dujailah was approached from the east. While still about a mile away, the 1-9th Gurkhas, which was leading battalion, halted and sent patrols forward. They found the Redoubt unoccupied. Our sensations may be imagined at walking over the position in the effort to take which we had failed so disastrously, and in such a costly manner, two months before. We now realised what an extraordinarily strong position it was. There were five tiers of fire-trenches up the slope, and very strong wire at its foot.

The whole of the Sinn position was now in our hands, or 'had been carried,' as appeared in General Gorringe's dispatch. The Turkish trenches and camps were left in a perfect sanitary condition, and it made one wonder at the time if a camp from which a British Army had retired, would have been cleaned up so well. It is, however, only fair to ourselves to state, that on all future occasions when old Turkish camps were occupied, they were found to be in a perfectly disgusting condition.

We expected shortly to be in Kut – now nothing but the empty shell of our former ambitions. It did not occur to anyone that the enemy would hold on to the Sunnaiyat position with his right flank thrown back so far, but this he did, against all efforts on our part, for nine months. Our cavalry, reconnoitring towards Kut, found it occupied, and retired, and so our line was adopted from Dujailah Redoubt to near Magasis.

The brigade bivouacked that night on the Redoubt, and next day the H.L.I. and 93rd were sent to occupy an outpost position, with the right of the 93rd on the Depression north-west of the Redoubt, and the left of the H.L.I. on the Redoubt itself. The 7th and 36th Brigades continued our line to the river bank. After completing the picquet trenches, our alignment was moved forward about a mile, and the position had to be re-dug. This period on outpost was not so

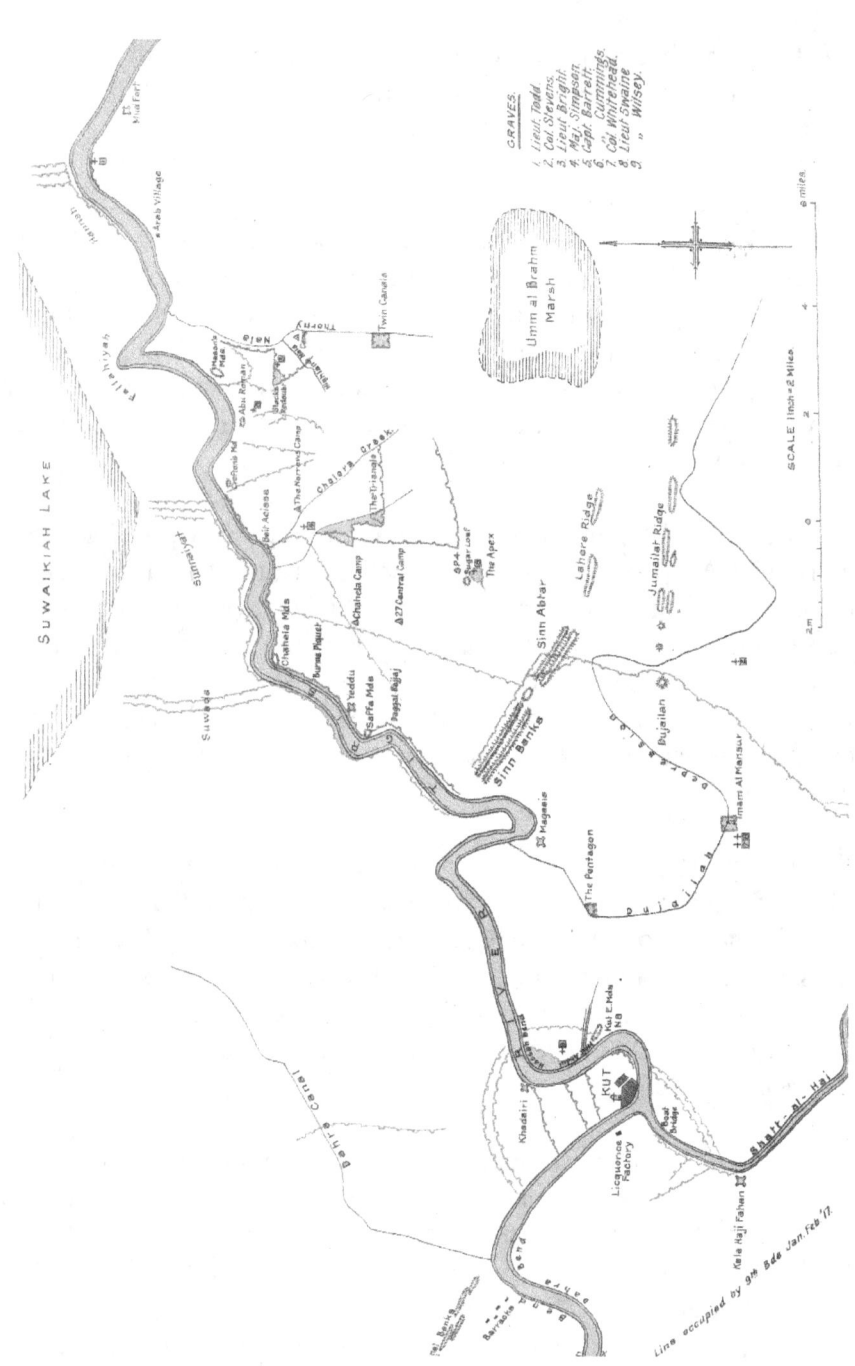

Sketch 7 Shumran to Twin Canals. Chapters VII, VIII and IX

unpleasant as it had been at S.P.4, chiefly because we had got away from the corpses, and the flies were consequently not so bad. Also a few large drafts enabled us to consider ourselves a regiment again, and to hold our heads a bit higher.

On 31 May, Colonel Whitehead rejoined, and took over command, and shortly after Lieutenant Smith arrived with a draft. Lieutenant Hodson, however, was lost for a time, as he was transferred to C.F.A. with jaundice. Major Morgan also went on semi-leave, and semi-dentistry, to Amara.

While in this line, the opportunity was taken of visiting the old battlefield of 8 March, and, as was mentioned before, it was found that all the graves had been reopened. It was never definitely discovered if this was done by Turks, or by jackals; but, as all the legs were exposed, and the boots taken, it appeared that the former were guilty.

The Arabs round this part of the world were expert thieves, equalling, if not surpassing, their confreres on the North-West Frontier. Many are the tales told of them, perhaps the most amusing being that of when they stole the sheep from S. and T. pen at Ali Gharbi, and, driving them to Sheikh Saad, resold them to the S. and T. there. Round our part of the world they chiefly stole horses, at which practice they were extraordinarily clever. One day we set a trap for them. Two A.T. carts containing 12 men covered with tarpaulins, and under the command of Jemadar Gulab Khan, were sent out aimlessly into the blue. They were soon spotted by the watchful Arabs, who cantered towards them. Unfortunately, our men uncovered themselves too soon, and, the range being too great for a galloping target, there were no results.

An expedition was being planned at this time against Gusab's Fort, an Arab stronghold some 12 miles south of Dujailah. As this would have entailed two long night marches, and a running fight during the intervening day, when the thermometer would have stood at about 120 degrees in the shade, no one was sorry when the expedition was given up.

Orders now came for the newly-raised 14th Division to relieve the 3rd Division, in order to let the latter recuperate behind. So back we had to go to the ground so full of dread memories, that we hated so much. As a place of rest, with its thicker vegetation, and consequently less dust, the forward area was infinitely preferable to the country east of Sinn.

During the evening of 17 June, the regiment was relieved by the 26th Punjabis, and marched to bivouacs some two miles back.

Next day, orders were received for half the battalion to relieve the 4th Gurkhas at Beit Aeissa picquet, and for the other half to act as water-party, and guard at a pump, and watering place north of Chahela. The regiment marched at 5 p.m., arriving at Chahela Camp at dusk. Here the left wing under Lieutenant Trevelyan remained as water-party, and the right wing, and Battalion Headquarters, with a guide from the 4th Gurkhas, marched on for Beit Aeissa picquet. As someone once remarked, there are two kinds of guides, the good and the bad. The bad guide says he knows the way, and does not; the good guide does not know the way, and says so. Ours was a bad one.

It was now pitch dark, and after wandering in the blue for some time, Colonel Whitehead decided to halt the battalion and let them bivouac, and to take on only sufficient men to relieve the 4th Gurkhas. Accordingly, Battalion Headquarters, with Lieutenant Wilsey and a few men, wandered on, and luckily struck the old Turkish trench of 17 April. This was easily recognisable from its battered condition, and the stench of corpses which emanated therefrom. Following it down, the picquet, which was where the trench met the river, was reached. It was 1 a.m. before the Gurkhas were relieved, and 3 a.m. before Battalion Headquarters arrived back at the regiment, Lieutenant Wilsey having been left temporarily in command at Beit Aeissa. Next day the remainder of the right wing, with Battalion Headquarters, rejoined the picquet.

Beit Aeissa picquet was a pestilential spot, perhaps the worst that the regiment ever found itself in during the war. It was more or less commanded by the Turkish picquets on the other bank, so that tents were not possible. The daily temperature had by now risen to about 120 degrees, so one can imagine how much higher it was in a dugout covered by a waterproof sheet. Every ditch around contained a pile of corpses, British and Turk. There were some even in the picquet itself. They were in the mummified condition that corpses always attain when left to dry in a strong sun, and their sweet, sickly odour pervaded the whole place. The flies were having the time of their lives. When one reflected that the fly one had just swallowed had probably lately arisen from the remains of that obese Turk just over the way, a sudden change in one's train of thought became necessary for internal peace.

The sand flies rendered sleep at night almost impossible. As the picquet was on the river bank, these pests were in especial abundance, and an ordinary mosquito curtain was no protection against them.

On 25 June, the regiment was relieved at Beit Aeissa by the H.L.I. and marched to Chahela camp. On the day previous to this, Lieutenant Haycraft went sick with dysentery, and Lieutenant Trevelyan took over the adjutancy.

The regiment moved from Chahela to S.P.4 on 2 July, and remained there for two months. One company, under Lieutenant Smith, was posted at S.P.5 on the road to Twin Canals, and, as Arabs raided round that part of the world, no one could move out without an escort of 10 rifles.

This was a time of inertia. The heat was very great, and the tentage very short, and, as nearly all the men were used up on duties, there were practically no parades. The getting of water and rations presented great difficulties, as rations had to be drawn from Twin Canals, and the water, at first from Abu Roman six miles away, and afterwards from the Narrows three miles away. Subadar Indar Singh, I.O.M., was wounded while commanding the escort to a water-party, which occasionally got shelled from the other bank. There was no fresh water for washing, but there were two wells, both extremely brackish.

Both officers and men suffered on account of the lack of fresh provisions. No fruit or vegetables were obtainable, and even potatoes went bad on the voyage upstream; the result was that that there were a great many cases of jaundice and pyorrhoea, though in this respect our regiment suffered less than any other unit in that area.

About this time a draft of P.M.s arrived from the 46th Punjabis, and Lieutenant Walters joined from our depot. On 26 June Lieutenant Hobday was invalided. He had been very unwell since March, but had managed to stick it out until the bad part of the hot weather.

Early in July, Major Morgan went on leave to India.

Lewis guns now arrived for the first time in Mesopotamia. Each double-company was given two guns, and Lieutenant Smith went through a course, and became regimental instructor.

In August, the Sheikh Saad – Sinn railway was in course of construction, and passed close to S.P.4. A line of blockhouses was dug, and garrisoned by the 93rd, and S.P.5. was abandoned.

At the end of August, machine guns were brigaded, and Lieutenant Wilsey went to command our section of the company so formed.

On 3 September, the 1-9th Gurkhas relieved us at S.P.4, and we went to the Narrows Camp, and took over picquet duties on the river bank, from Beit Aeissa to Daqq al Hajjaj. Shortly after they had relieved us, the 1-9th returned to India. This greatly raised the idea that other regiments would also be going, though none went except the 89th Punjabis, from the 7th Brigade. Certain other changes, however, took place in the division. The 7th Brigade was made complete by the arrival of the 91st Punjabis, and 2-7th Gurkhas, the latter replacing the 128th Pioneers. In the 8th Brigade, the 124th Baluchis relieved the 4th Rajputs, which regiment, for the last few months, had taken the place of the 2nd Rajputs. In our brigade, the 105th Mahratta Light Infantry relieved the 1-9th Gurkhas. More drafts arrived at this time, including one from the Burma Military Police, also some officers, namely, 2nd Lieutenants Oatway, and Coffey, I.A.R.O., and Challen, 72nd Punjabis. Lieutenant Pegg also joined from the depot.

The Narrows Camp was about 1,000 yards from the river, near the edge of the Beit Aeissa battlefield, and well within range of the Turkish guns. For two days the camp was shelled, but with fortunately little damage. Later in September the river picquets were strengthened, and the battalion on duty moved their headquarters to a new camp called 27 Central, about three miles south-west of the Narrows, and an elaborate system of communication trenches between the river picquets was dug.

On 4 October, Major Morgan and Lieutenant Haycraft rejoined the battalion from India, and at the same time the platoon organisation was adopted, No. 1 D.C. becoming A Company, and so on. The war establishment of Indian units was still the same as it had been before the war, but we never actually reached full strength, and so, while each company was divided into four platoons, there were only sufficient men to allow two sections in each platoon. It was not until a year later that the complete four sections per platoon were formed.

Major Morgan took over command of A Company, Lieutenant Haycraft that of B, Lieutenant Pegg C, and Lieutenant Walters D Company, Lieutenant Trevelyan remaining as adjutant.

On 12 October, the regiment returned from river-picquet duty to the Narrows Camp. By this time the conditions of life were steadily improving. Fresh meat and potatoes were occasionally issued, and these, supplemented by the sand grouse, which abounded in this part of the world, made meals a relish instead of a duty. The light railway, too, enabled a fairly regular supply of canteen stores to be brought from Sheikh Saad.

Now that the weather was getting cooler, training in a mild form commenced, mild because every other night was spent in digging communication trenches between the river picquets. These fatigues were no light task. The digging place was generally about three miles from camp, and the work took about four hours, commencing at 7 p.m. As the sound of the work could always be heard on the other bank, the Turk usually did his best to enliven the proceedings.

On 21 October, B and D Companies went to a permanent digging camp behind Safa picquet, where they relieved A and C Companies. They remained there until the regiment's next turn for picquet duty came round, on 9 November.

These periods in river picquets were really rather popular among all ranks. The regiment engaged on them was excused all fatigues, and, though the duties by night were heavy, the men had the whole of the day to themselves, only a small observation post being left in the picquet. But better than all this, of course, to the sepoy's mind, was the abundance of water.

Some picquets were very much more popular than others, the best being that at Sinn Banks. Here the majority of the men lived in the support, between the canal banks, about a mile-and-a-half from the river. They were not under observation there, and such luxuries as tents, and football were permissible.

The picquets at Safa and Chahela were also pleasant, as here again one was not under observation in the lee of the mounds, and greater freedom was possible.

The only duties were observation by night to prevent a crossing of the river, and by day, the expenditure of a sufficient number of rounds to fulfil the conditions of the question that the staff informed us we should be perpetually asking ourselves, namely, 'Am I as offensive as I possibly can be?' This injunction, coming from the staff, caused a lot of dry, caustic, and sometimes bitter amusement among the mere regimental officers, especially those who had been present in the spring campaign.

On 21 November, the regiment was relieved in river picquets by the 1-1st Gurkhas, and returned to the Narrows Camp.

Chapter VIII

Operations in The Mahomed Abdul Hassan Bend, December 1916 – January 1917

Certain indications of activity, which people had learnt from experience to discern from afar, showed that something was in the wind. Urgent enquiries were being made regarding kit and equipment; scales of clothing were issued, which, in their generosity, almost equalled what had been received in France; the amount of transport allotted to units was very minutely laid down. All this, while very ominous, had a reassuring effect. There appeared to be a brain working behind it all – a brain capable of making a "bandobast," and seeing it through. Things were not being done in the haphazard, go-as-you-please style of the preceding spring.

Our surmises soon proved to be correct. Another had assumed command in place of the many generals who had followed each other downstream earlier in the year – General Sir Stanley Maude, who afterwards proved himself to be one of the ablest strategical, and administrative generals England has produced, was now in command.

Force D had also undergone considerable reorganisation. The 3rd and 7th Divisions were now united in the 1st Corps, under General Cobbe, while the 13th and 14th Divisions became the 3rd Corps under General Marshall. Whether the fact that there was no 2nd Corps deceived the Turk, or not, was never discovered.

Though the usual wild conjectures were repeated, no one dreamt that our ultimate objective was to be Baghdad. The capture of Kut, perhaps, and the consequent recovery of a little of our lost prestige, was all that people speculated on at that time.

The disposition of our forces in Mesopotamia at this period was as follows. The 7th Division was still in front of Sunnaiyat. The 14th

Division was in the forward area on the right bank, beyond Sinn, with the 8th Brigade of the 3rd Division in support at Sinn Abiar. Our brigade had one battalion on river picquets, between Sinn and Beit Aeissa, with the other battalions in support, at the Narrows, while the 7th Brigade was concentrated at Highland Nala. The 13th Division was coming upstream from Amara, where it had spent the hot weather, and was slowly collecting round Twin Canals. The 14th Division had advanced slightly in the forward area, and held the four strongpoints, Dujailah, Imam al Mansur, the Pentagon, and Magasis (Sketch No. 7).

On 10 December, the 7th relieved the 9th Brigade, and the latter concentrated at Highland Nala, where Lieutenant Swaine, who had left us in France, rejoined the regiment. The first rain of the cold weather had set in just before our march to Highland Nala, and the place was a sea of mud when we arrived. Stack's Redoubt, and the Lunette were still quite recognisable, also Bright's grave, on which we erected a cross.

The 13th Division, having concentrated, was now slowly moving forward, leaving their tents standing at Twin Canals to deceive the enemy.

Ours being now the furthest division from the Turk, everyone thought that it would be the last to be engaged. It was actually the first to take part in the serious portion of the campaign that followed.

Dummy bombardments, to engage the enemy reserves, were kept up on Sunnaiyat, and on the night of 12 December, the 13th and 14th Divisions crossed the Shatt al Hai, and, wheeling northwards, dug in before the Hai Bridgehead defences. At 1 p.m. on Sunday 17th, the 9th Brigade received orders to march westwards in an hour's time. We unfortunately had to leave behind Lieutenant Pegg, who was suffering from jaundice, and was transferred to C.F.A.

The other regiments of the brigade spent the night at Sinn Abtar, which was reached after dark, but the 93rd had to proceed to bivouacs at Devizes Bridge, some two miles further on. It was 1 a.m. before the men were finally able to turn in.

Next morning the H.L.I. and 93rd concentrated in the Dujailah Depression, just south of the Pentagon, while the 1-1st Gurkhas, and 105th Mahrattas relieved the 8th Brigade in a picquet line they had taken up round the Mahomed Abdul Hassan Bend, from No. 8 on the river bank, to the Pentagon (Sketch No. 7). On relief, the 8th Brigade continued the line from the right of the 9th Brigade at the Pentagon, to the river bank north of it, thus hemming the Turks into the Bend, where they were strongly entrenched. Their reasons for being so were twofold. Firstly, the possession by us of this bend would give our guns complete command of the Kut peninsula. Secondly, by holding the entrance of the Triple Nalas, they could flood the low-lying country to the south as soon as the river was high enough, and so imperil our communications with the 13th and 14th Divisions, and very likely swamp the Sheikh Saad – Sinn railway, which was now being prolonged towards Atab. For similar reasons it was necessary for us to evict them from the Bend.

Beyond a little shelling, and the return of the machine gun personnel, who had been relieved by the 133rd British Machine Gun Company, nothing eventful happened until 23 December, when the 93rd relieved the 1-1st Gurkhas in the picquet line from the Pentagon, to a point halfway between this and N8. Just before this, General Campbell had been wounded by a bullet through the arm, and Colonel Anderson, 1-1st Gurkhas, officiated for him in his absence.

An isolated redoubt had been built at K9 in front of our line (Sketch No. 8) and at night A Company, under Major Morgan, relieved the 1-1st Gurkha company there. A Company split up shortly afterwards, and held a post at M5A as well as K9.

The weather had now taken a turn for the worse, and up to the end of our share in the operations (13 January) there was almost continuous rain, drizzle, or mist.

On 24 December, Lieutenant Oatway went to C.F.A. with jaundice, and next night, an officer's patrol, under Lieutenant Haycraft, failed to find any enemy between K9 and the Turkish front line. As a result of this, B Company was ordered to establish three platoon posts, called A, B, and C Posts, six hundred yards in front of the K9 – M5A line. This was successfully done before daylight, while fatigues from the 105th Mahrattas joined the posts up with the rear by communication trenches. Meanwhile other companies of the 93rd had been improving the lateral communication between K9 and MDA, these two posts still being garrisoned by A Company, and from thence towards the 1-1st Gurkhas at Kut East Mounds.

Next night A, B, and C Posts were joined up by a lateral fire-trench. When this was complete, the 105th Mahrattas relieved A and B Companies, which returned, through a veritable downpour, to what had now become the reserve line.

From here nightly fatigue parties dug communication trenches forward from A, B, and C Posts, to lunettes called A, B, and C, T-heads, respectively. These were again joined up by lateral fire-trenches. On our right the 8th Brigade carried on a similar series of works up to the river bank. Thus passed the most miserable Christmas week that the regiment had spent on service. Incessant rain, lack of tents (there was none even for the mess), combined with sleepless nights on working parties, under continuous sniping, held none of the joys one expects at Christmas time.

But the most ticklish part of the digging operations was yet to come, i.e. joining C T-head with Kut East Mounds.

It will be seen from Sketch No. 8 that our line from C T-head to the left ran parallel to, and about 150 yards away from, the Turkish front line. To the right it diverged away from the enemy trench. The 8th Brigade had now taken over A and B T-heads from us, and the 9th Brigade was concentrated between C T-head and Kut East Mounds, the 105th Mahrattas occupying the former, and the 1-1st Gurkhas the latter. It fell to the lot of the 93rd to join these two up with a lateral fire-trench. The working party was detailed from D Company, to be

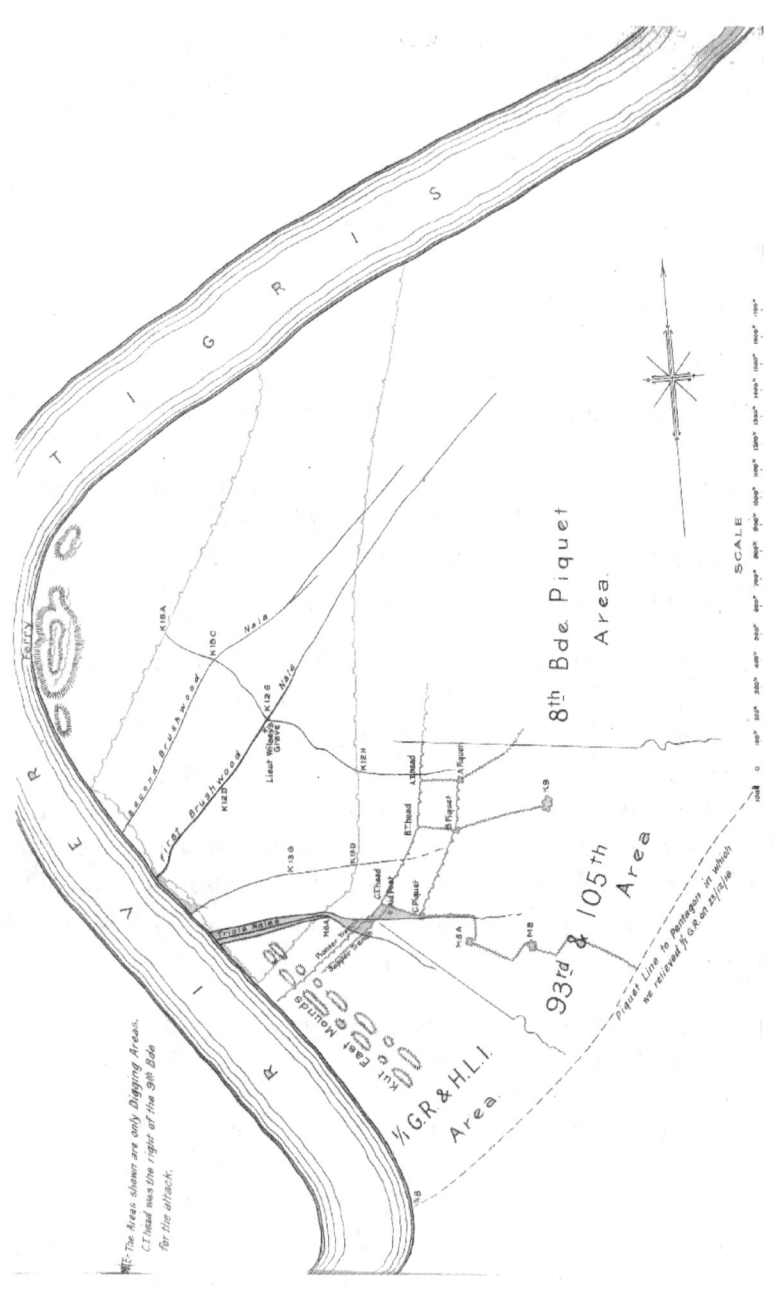

Sketch 8 Mahomed Abdul Hassan Bend. Chapter VIII

relieved by B Company at midnight. The night was cloudy, but the moon was fairly full, and, directly the men filed out from C T-head to extend on their work, they were met by a hail of bullets from the Turkish trenches only 150 yards away. Several attempts were made, during one of which Lieutenant Walters was wounded in the hand. Our casualties were steadily mounting up, and Colonel Whitehead, who had arrived on the scene, and who exhibited the most complete contempt for death in wandering up and down the line, decided to send out only enough men to dig one bay at a time. In this way the work was very slow, and not nearly complete by morning, by which time we had suffered considerable casualties. The work done like this was much too expensive in lives, and eventually it was completed by the 34th Pioneers, who sapped it with marmooties.

On 7 January, news arrived that Lieutenant Haycraft had been awarded the M.C. for the Kut Relief operations.

Dummy bombardments had been taking place for some time on the Turkish line, and it was very evident that the enemy were having a thin time of it.

On the 8th, general orders for the attack were issued. The 9th Brigade was to attack from C T-head to the river, the order of attack, from right to left, being the 93rd, 105th Mahrattas, and two companies 1-1st Gurkhas, with the remaining two companies of the 1-1st Gurkhas, and the H.L.I. in reserve. Immediately on the right of the 93rd, the Manchesters and 59th Rifles, of the 8th Brigade, were to attack from C T-head exclusive to B T-head.

The orders for getting into position, and for the bombardment, et cetera, were most minute, but are not worth repeating as they will all come out in the tale that follows.

D Company was now commanded by Lieutenant Wilsey, Lieutenant Walters having been transferred to C.F.A. after his wound, while in C Company Lieutenant Smith had replaced Lieutenant Pegg. A and B Companies were still commanded by Major Morgan, and

Lieutenant Haycraft, respectively. Of the other officers, Lieutenant Trevelyan was adjutant, Lieutenant Challen was with B Company, while Lieutenants Hodson and Coffey remained behind as quartermaster and transport officer respectively. B and D were to be the attacking companies, with C in support, and A in reserve. B and D Companies were to attack in four lines, a platoon of B on the right, and D on the left, being in each line. C Company was to follow in two lines, with A in reserve.

The first objective of the 93rd was the Turkish front line between K13D, and the Triple Nalas (Sketch No. 8), and, after swinging round, the second objective was the nala between K13D and K13G. No advance was to be made beyond this line until the receipt of fresh orders. The remainder of our brigade would swing round with the 93rd and occupy the continuation of the nala K13D, K13G, to the river bank, while the 8th Brigade would capture the front line, and then bomb up the nala KI2H, K12G.

During the morning of 8 January, A Company relieved the H.L.I. in C T-head, and the latter concentrated in M5, and MD5A. After dark the remaining companies marched independently in the order D, B, C, via the communication trench M5, M5A, C, C T-head. D and B Companies filed into Pioneer Trench, relieving A Company, which retired towards C picquet, while C Company occupied Sapper Trench.

As will be seen in the orders for the attack, it was necessary for each platoon of B and D Companies to cover the whole front of its company. The difficulty of this was obviated, when originally marching off, by putting one man of each platoon in each four, thus, when they filed into Pioneer Trench, every fourth man belonged to the same platoon, and so each platoon was distributed along the whole front of its Company.

At dusk on the 8th, a heavy mist came up, in spite of which the rather difficult manoeuvre of getting into position was accomplished without a hitch. At 9 p.m. ammunition, bombs, and tools were drawn from Battalion Headquarters, situated near the aid post, and steps were cut through the parapet for our exit next morning.

The men were packed like sardines in Pioneer Trench. Sleep even in a feather bed would be fitful the night before an attack; under these conditions it was impossible; moreover, the intermittent rat-tat-tat of enemy machine guns added to the general uneasiness. There is a nasty sinking feeling in the pit of the stomach when you hear a machine gun spitting bullets from the exact point on which you, yourself, are going to advance next morning. You find yourself indulging in mental calculations as to how far apart the bullets from a traversing machine gun are spaced, and the chances a man two feet wide has of meeting a space, and not a bullet. If you have not yet been in action, you wonder what it feels like to be wounded; if you have, visions of some ghastly wounds that you have seen somewhere previously, cross your mind. With a supreme mental effort, you dismiss the thought, and force your mind to think of pleasant things, happy days spent in England – anything to keep the nightmare away. Presently that cursed machine gun, or the blast of a shell, recalls tomorrow's business, and so the cycle of thought goes on, until, mercifully, dawn dispels it with its light. This dawn broke through the same heavy mist of the night before, to the music of distant bombardments at Sunnaiyat, and the Hai Bridgehead, where efforts were being made to distract the enemy's attention from our front.

Zero hour was to be at 8.45 a.m., and the bombardment was to start at 7.45 a.m., with a lull at zero minus 10 minutes, until zero. The bombardment would recommence at zero, and continue until zero plus 15 minutes (i.e. 9 a.m.) when fire ceased. At zero plus 13 minutes (8.58 a.m.) the front line was to leave our trench, and close with the enemy as the bombardment stopped.

At about 8 a.m. officers collected near the aid post for breakfast – a somewhat cheerless meal. It is unpleasant looking round a circle of friends, and knowing that some of the number are spending their last half-hour on earth. One wonders if one is among the latter – a thought which recurs persistently, and one which must be as persistently checked. Faces look pinched, and strained on these occasions, there is an unnatural glitter in the eyes, the conversation is forced, and the slightest humour evokes an exaggerated laugh.

During the preliminary bombardment one of our own 4.5 inch shells fell in the trench occupied by B Company, knocking out the whole bay; this, however, was the only case of a short burst that day.

At last the time for action drew near. The hour's bombardment was finished, and, after the lull, the final 15 minutes of hell was let loose. At 8.58 a.m. exactly, our front line leapt from Pioneer Trench, and, halting a minute in no-man's land to allow the rear lines to close up, crossed the enemy's wire as the bombardment ceased, jumped into the enemy's trench, and either bayonetted, or captured the occupants. They were crouching down to escape our bombardment, and our arrival was too sudden to give them time to recover.

The Turkish line had been blown to pieces by our guns, and large lengths of it bore no resemblance to a trench at all, while numerous corpses, unearthed from their graves by our shells, testified to the efficiency of the previous dummy bombardments. The wire was cut to such an extent that it offered no obstacle to our advance.

Swinging round immediately, the leading companies occupied the nala K13D – K13G, which was found to be only about 18 inches deep. Heavy enemy rifle and machine gun fire now opened from the direction of Brushwood Nala. This, thanks to the mist, was not too accurate, but it necessitated our digging in as quickly as possible.

At the commencement of the attack, Colonel Whitehead received a nasty shell wound in the shoulder. He immediately had it bound up, and resumed command of the regiment within 10 minutes.

The units on our right and left were equally successful. The 105th Mahrattas were soon in continuation of our left, while the Manchesters had reached the enemy front line on our right from K13D northwards. The 59th Rifles, however, who were supposed to come up on the right of the Manchesters, failed to arrive. The result was an immediate counter-attack by the Turks via K12G – K12H, which, taking the Manchesters' exposed flank unawares, rolled it up.

Lieutenant Swaine, seeing that the Manchesters were in difficulties, dashed off alone to their assistance. We never saw him alive again. He was evidently killed by a bomb, for his remains were identified two days later, and buried at Imam al Mansur.

The Manchesters retired in some disorder, leaving A Company, under Major Morgan,[6] which had now arrived at K13D, to stem the rush. Had A Company not stood firm, the whole line would have gone. It did not take the Manchesters long to return. Reforming in no-man's land in a most gallant manner, they again advanced, and ousted the Turk. They held on to that flank like grim death all day with fluctuating fortunes.

The 1-1st Gurkhas, on the river bank, experienced some difficulties at first, but drew level later. The mist continued all day, making aeroplane cooperation impossible, and, beyond the fluctuations of the bombing duel on our right, there was no change in the situation by dusk, when the two companies of the 1-1st Gurkhas, which had been in reserve, relieved the Manchesters on our right. After dark the front was wired in by the sappers, but the night passed uneventfully, and patrols to the north-west revealed no enemy for at least 500 yards. On the right, where the Gurkhas had relieved the Manchesters, peace also reigned, showing that the Turks had retired up the nala towards K12G.

10 January broke a beautifully clear day, and B and D Companies were sent forward to occupy the First Brushwood Nala. This necessitated crossing some 800 yards in successive waves, which were fairly severely shelled by enemy guns on the left bank, causing

---

[6] Mr Candler in *Long Road to Baghdad* is incorrect as regards this part of the action. The Manchesters were on the right of the 93rd, and, except for the above incident, contact was maintained between the two regiments all day. The H.L.I. never bombed up to the Manchesters, nor were they employed at all on 9 January.

some casualties. B and D Companies occupied the First Brushwood Nala from K12G to K12D, with the 105th Mahrattas on the left. A bombing block was made up the nala K12G – KI5C, but patrols to the front drew fire from the enemy's second line.

The First Brushwood Nala was about five feet deep, four feet broad, and nearly straight – a fact which brought disaster on us the next day. The front was covered with thick undergrowth, through which the Turkish second line trenches to our front were invisible.

We were left in peace most of the day, during which too much time was spent in making ourselves comfortable, and too little in traversing the nala – a negligence which cost us dear later. The nala from K12G to K12H, which was cleared of corpses during the day, was a ghastly sight. All the Turkish counter-attacks of the previous day had come down this nala, on which our guns had been repeatedly concentrated. The bodies of British and Turk, piled thick and deep, were torn by the terrible wounds caused by shell fire; and the enemy, when retiring, had stripped them naked of clothing and boots.

In the evening a patrol under Lieutenant Challen found the Second Brushwood Nala unoccupied, but this turned out to be only a shallow depression some three feet across, and one foot deep. Later, according to orders, two platoon posts were established in the Second Brushwood Nala to assist the 8th Brigade, which had orders to make an attempt to take KI5A from the north-east. The H.L.I. were also ordered to co-operate by advancing up the nala K12G – KI5A.

This was a night of alarms and disturbances, bursts of fire and thudding of bombs, all made more awesome by the bright light from the brushwood, which the Turks had lit to show up their front. On 11 January dawn broke on a murky day, and K15A still remained in the hands of the Turks.

The enemy were now hemmed into the top of the bend, along their second line, which skirted some low sand hills along the river bank, bristling with machine gun emplacements. It was again fairly misty, and aeroplanes reported that the Turkish ferry at the top of the bend was very busy.

The "powers-that-be" presumed that the Turk was evacuating the bend – a very natural presumption had they been dealing with a normal enemy instead of the Turk. The 9th Brigade was ordered to attack from the south-east, and the 8th Brigade from the east. The 9th Brigade attack was to be done by the H.L.I. and 93rd. The H.L.I. were to advance in four lines, with the 93rd echeloned on their right rear.

On receipt of these orders the H.L.I. filed through us to our left in Brushwood Nala, and we closed on the right. Meanwhile Battalion Headquarters, with A and C Companies, which up to the present had remained in the Triple Nalas, arrived, and A Company took the place of B, which had suffered very badly in N.C.O.s. The order of companies from left to right in the First Brushwood Nala was now D, A, B, C.

The bombardment was very curtailed, many batteries not having even registered, owing to the shortness of the notice given. In spite of this the only bar to victory was the fact that the enemy were not evacuating the bend, but bringing across another regiment (three battalions) to relieve the one already there. We therefore had to deal with twice as many enemy as there were before.

By the time our D Company had left the First Brushwood Nala, the leading company of the H.L.I. were near the Turks, who suddenly rose in swarms, and advanced to meet them. In the hand-to-hand struggle which ensued the H.L.I. were bested through numerical inferiority, and fell back in confusion on the First Brushwood Nala, taking our D Company with them.

Things now looked very black. It appeared as if the Turks were going to follow up the H.L.I. retirement, while a heavy bombardment of enemy 5.9 inch guns opened on the First Brushwood Nala. These guns were firing from the other side of Kut, and so caught us in complete enfilade, and, the nala being wide and straight, their work of destruction was easy. After a while the nala had the appearance of a scene of massacre – and one of a particularly brutal character, where most of the victims lay torn and bleeding, but not yet dead. Further description is unnecessary.

Colonel Whitehead, who had watched the attack from a very exposed position, fell, shot through the body. He knew he was done for, and said goodbye to all officers as he was carried away. It was one of the most inspiring moments of the regiment's history. Stripped to the waist, except for the bloodstained bandages, he lay paralysed on a stretcher. As the bearers carried him away he encouraged the men with words, in a voice still strong enough to be heard above the din of battle.

Lieutenant Challen, who had been wounded in the leg in no-man's land, was very gallantly rescued by Subadar Karam Dad and No. 2569 Havildar Chanan Shah, for which act these two afterwards received the I.O.M. Lieutenant Wilsey and Subadar Fazal Dad were both killed by shell fire, and Jemadar Harnam Singh was wounded. The former was buried at the junction of the nala KI5A – K12H with the First Brushwood Nala, where his grave was recognised untouched 18 months later.

Luckily the Turks never followed up the retirement of the H.L.I. properly. Our gunners say that when they got wind of what was happening, they put down such a barrage in front of the Turkish second line, that no attacking enemy could have got through it. Be that as it may, our attention was fully occupied by the bombardment on us, and we heard nothing of it. Towards evening the fire stopped, the maimed and killed were disposed of, and patrols by night brought in many wounded who had lain out in the open all day.

This completed our active participation in the Mahomed Abdul Hassan Bend operations, during which the regiment lost 3 British officers killed, 2 wounded, and 183 casualties of other ranks, or 37 percent of the numbers engaged.

Next morning, we were relieved by the 105th Mahrattas, and retired to brigade reserve at K13D, where the news that we were expecting was received – that Colonel Whitehead had died of wounds in hospital. He was buried at Imam al Mansur, and once more the earth covered the remains of a gallant officer, brave in war and gentle in instinct. He had joined the regiment when they were at their lowest ebb of depression, after an unsuccessful campaign. He brought them through a terrible hot weather, himself in no condition to stand it. Finally, he led the regiment into action, inspiring them by his own splendid example of coolness under fire, and died in the attempt. Could any man have done more?

While in brigade reserve we received a message from the 8th Brigade, thanking us for the assistance we had rendered to the Manchesters during the counter-attack on 9 January.

Major Morgan now, for the second time, commanded the regiment.

The scene near Battalion Headquarters at K13D was a gruesome one. All the killed of both attacks were laid out in rows for identification, and men were engaged in trying to fit odd heads and limbs on to bodies lacking them. No one was sorry to leave the place, when, during the night of 14 January, the 9th Brigade was relieved by the 7th Brigade.

During these operations the 7th Brigade had been sitting in river picquets, and the relief took place in driblets. First, the 2-7th Gurkhas relieved the 105th Mahrattas in Brushwood Nala, and the latter came to brigade reserve. Thus our regiment was released, and marched to the Pentagon, arriving there after midnight. Here we found a liberal rum ration and hot mince pies – a thoughtful provision by our quartermaster, Lieutenant Hodson. It had by now become a habit among officers in the regiment to expect "Father" to provide some luxury out of the ordinary at the conclusion of any nasty piece of work. Sometimes, of course, he had nothing to offer; but there was always his cheerful, red face to be seen again – an excellent tonic for jaded nerves.

Next day, we relieved the 27th Punjabis in river picquets from Magasis to the Mahomed Abdul Hassan Bend.

The arrival of some drafts at this period replenished our depleted numbers. Lieutenant Pegg also rejoined from hospital, and 2nd Lieutenant Scott arrived as a reinforcement from the 72nd Punjabis.

Another attack on the Turkish line in the Mahomed Abdul Hassan Bend, to be made by the 7th Brigade, was ordered for the morning of 18 January. This never came off, as patrols discovered that the bend had been evacuated during the night. Thus the operations closed, and on 10 January, the 93rd were relieved by the Connaught Rangers, and marched to Sinn Abtar, where, at a parade of the 8th and 9th Brigades, General Maude presented awards for the operations.

Chapter IX
Baghdad

While the brigade was at Sinn Abtar, the H.L.I., who had suffered very badly in officers on 11 January, was relieved by the 2nd Dorset Regiment. We never again met the H.L.I., who had been in the brigade since 1914. They afterwards joined the 17th Division, which was formed some six months later, and, although they made great efforts to return to the 3rd Division, at the time the latter was under orders for Palestine, they were unsuccessful.

We were not left long in rest at Sinn Abtar. On 21 January, the brigade, under the command of General Campbell, who had just rejoined, marched to bivouacs some two miles west of Bassouia. After the sedentary life that had been led in the Mahomed Abdul Hassan Bend, this was a long and trying march, and, before we could really settle into bivouacs, the rain set in. During the march, 2nd Lieutenant Rigg joined as a reinforcement from the 91st Punjabis.

The position of affairs in this new area was as follows. It will be remembered that the 13th and 14th Divisions had crossed the Hai in December. They had then swung northwards, and came up against the enemy's bridgehead defences on both banks of the mouth of the Hai. Here they remained more or less inactive while the 3rd Division cleared the Mahomed Abdul Hassan Bend. This was now complete, and the turn of the 13th and 14th Divisions had come.

In order to protect their rear from Arabs, or an enveloping movement by the Turks, the 9th Brigade, followed shortly afterwards by the 8th Brigade, moved down to occupy a picquet line from Bassouia in a north-westerly direction. This line was already dug, and was composed of a system of strongly wired redoubts, with alternating lunettes.

The day after our arrival, the 1-1st Gurkhas and 105th Mahrattas occupied this line, with the Dorsets and 93rd in reserve. A few days later Lieutenant Oatway rejoined from hospital, and took over command of D Company. After a short spell of rain, the weather turned fine and cold, with sharp frosts by night.

On 25 January, the Hai Bridgehead operations commenced with an attack west of the Hai. It is unnecessary to attempt to describe these operations in detail, as this, after all, is a purely regimental history, and our part in the action was quite subsidiary. Suffice it to say that the Turk was gradually driven back from trench to trench by a series of small and local attacks, first on one side of the Hai, and then on the other, until by 8 February the whole of the ground east of the Hai was in our hands.

The real meaning of these operations was not apparent at the time. It must be remembered that no one definitely realised that Baghdad was to be the ultimate objective. It was not the acquisition of a few yards of enemy trench system that General Maude had in mind, but the gradual killing off of as many Turks as possible. By calculations based on reports which were collected after all attacks, as to the number of corpses seen, he was able to gauge the breaking point of the enemy's strength, and so, at the critical moment, deal the hammer-blow which revealed the object he had in view. All the operations undertaken by General Maude were enveloped in the most profound secrecy. It was said that even his most intimate staff officers were totally ignorant of what his real intentions were.

One must not, however, lose sight of the fact that, even if full allowance is made for the skilful handling of this campaign, it would not have succeeded but for two things. These were, firstly, the great improvement that had taken place in the method of transport, and secondly the dry season we were favoured with.

After the Mesopotamian scandals, money had poured into the country. Whereas in the spring of 1916 the fastest moving transport vehicle was the A.T. cart, in 1917 the country was scoured by convoys of Ford vans; a light railway connected Sheikh Saad to within a few miles of the fighting line; and a fleet of large transport steamers, and luxuriant hospital ships, plied between Basra and the advanced base. While General Aylmer could not maintain his force at Dujailah after the battle for more than a day, General Maude could now permanently keep three divisions beyond the Hai, supplied, not only with the necessities of life, but with luxuries undreamt of before, though the river base – Sheikh Saad – of both generals was the same. A man wounded in the Dahra Bend operations could be conveyed to a splendidly fitted hospital boat in half the time that it would have taken to convey a man wounded at Beit Aeissa to the bare deck of a river barge, though the distance was four times as great.

After the middle of January, the spring of 1917 was comparatively dry, and in no other way could fortune have favoured us better. Had it been necessary to fight an overflowing river, and a rain-sodden terrain, as well as the Turk, there can be little doubt that the British would not have entered Baghdad in March.

By 15 February, the only remaining Turks on the right bank were hemmed into the bend west of the Liquorice Factory, where a final attack brought us in 2,000 prisoners, and the possession of the whole of the Dahra Bend. We had previously relieved the 2-2nd Gurkhas, of the 14th Division, in the picquet line west of the 105th Mahrattas, and on 11 February, moved forward and relieved the North Stafford Regiment, of the 13th Division, in a new line of picquets, which prolonged the old one still further to the west.

While in this line, Major Haughton (who, it will be remembered, had been wounded at Beit Aeissa, and invalided to England) rejoined, and assumed command, while Major Morgan, who had been suffering from lumbago, took the opportunity of going to Amara for treatment. Second Lieutenants Lalor and Pearson also joined the regiment at this time as reinforcements.

As in all other matters, the system of filling up the wastages of battle was most efficient in the Baghdad campaign. While the 3rd Division was engaged in the Mahomed Abdul Hassan Bend, only reinforcements for that division were allowed up stream. The result was that, almost immediately after the operations, the regiment was filled up to its fighting strength again. This led everyone to believe that our brigade might be called upon to help the 3rd Corps in the Dahra Bend.

However, the 13th and 14th Divisions were able to cope with the work in hand without assistance, and we were given breathing space to bring our new drafts into line.

On the 15th, orders were received to move our picquet line some 2,000 yards forward by night, on a compass bearing. It was intensely dark when we commenced putting out these picquets, which were dropped from the regiment as it advanced on the bearing. Owing to a mistake at the starting point, it was found that the alignment was incorrect after all the picquets had been detailed, and this necessitated the readjustment of the line by night. This difficult proceeding caused hopeless confusion, and it was found next morning that some picquets were firing into the backs of others. A heavy downpour, which commenced at midnight, before our trenches were half completed, added to the general discomfort.

The right half of the picquet line was on low ground, and now that the weather had taken a turn for the worse, the surrounding vicinity soon became sodden, and uncomfortable. On the afternoon of 16 February a hailstorm set in such as we had never before experienced. The hailstones were as big as large marbles, and they came down in sheets. In 10 minutes the ground was white, and the trenches and dugouts were flush with water from the thawing hail.

On the 18th, we were relieved by a regiment of the 13th Division, and marched back to Bassouia. Here rumour was rife as to our next destination, the general idea being that the brigade would go to Sunnaiyat to help the 7th Division. This was actually done by the 8th Brigade, and next day our brigade returned to the picquet line they had just vacated.

It was now obvious that an attempt was to be made to cross the Tigris. This was done during the early morning of 23 February, with the utmost secrecy, by the Norfolks, 2-9th, and 1-2nd Gurkhas. The spot at which the crossing was made is marked on Sketch No. 7 with a X. A party was first of all rowed across in pontoons. These surprised and scuppered the Turkish picquets, who must have been asleep, and held the bank while a bridge was thrown across. Our infantry was soon over, and drove the enemy beyond the banks of the old Nahrwan Canal, thus letting our cavalry through.

Simultaneously the 7th Division attacked the Sunnaiyat position, from where the Turks, threatened now in the rear by the Shumran crossing, were soon fleeing in disorder. During the night, through some mistake, they got past our cavalry screen north of Shumran, and retreated towards Imam Mahdi, the 13th and 14th Divisions soon taking up the pursuit (Sketch No. 9).

On 26 February, the 9th Brigade concentrated, and bivouacked at the bridge at which the crossing had been made. It was a miserable night of intense rain, and we were a sodden collection of individuals next morning. At dawn, the brigade crossed, and marched to the western end of the Shumran Bend, where the 8th Brigade were found already assembled. This was the first time that the regiment had set foot on the left bank of the Tigris since 15 January 1916.

We anticipated continuing the march that night, and taking part in the pursuit, but our expectations were not fulfilled. Instead, orders came for the 9th Brigade to take up an outpost line, with their right on the eastern end of the Shumran Bend.

The regiment remained in this line until 4 March, when the 93rd were relieved by the 105th Mahrattas, and the former returned to brigade reserve. During this time a draft arrived from the 72nd Punjabis, and Major Morgan returned from Amara.

The other regiments of the brigade were moving gradually up stream, and on 7 March, B and D Companies moved to Imam Mahdi (Sketch No. 9), where they relieved two companies of the 1-1st Gurkhas. The remainder of the battalion joined this detachment next day, and four days later the regiment marched up stream.

The first night's halt was at Ash, where news of the fall of Baghdad was received, and the next day we marched to Aziziyah, finding the remainder of the brigade concentrated there in bivouacs. From Aziziyah the brigade marched by daily stages, the detail of which is given below. Some of these marches were fairly trying, but, until our arrival at Baghdad, the weather was moderately cool, and there was always the inestimable advantage of having the river to bivouac beside.

On 16 March, the famous Arch of Ctesiphon was passed, where Townshend's force had met its fate 18 months before; and next day the brigade entered Baghdad.

Expectations differ according to the conditions in which you have previously lived. Little luxuries that have been withheld will always appear desirous out of all proportion to the delight they give on attainment. During the long march up to Baghdad probably everyone had beguiled the hours with anticipatory thoughts of all that awaited them. A house to live in, a bed to sleep in, and green and shady trees to rest eyes grown weary with the strain of searching for something – in a limitless expanse of nothing.

The first sign of any fulfilment of their hopes was when the brigade reached Himaidi, on the bend of the river south of Baghdad. Here groves of palm trees fringe the river bank – drab and dust-laden, but trees for all that – while to the north the date gardens encircling Baghdad come into view. Countless Arab boys, selling the most luscious green lettuces, greeted the column as it entered these suburban gardens, and our spirits rose high in anticipation.

Of all the famous cities of the East, Baghdad was one of the least known before the war. The name, in consequence, conjured up visions of wonderful eastern colour, and splendour. It was a rude shock, as we marched through the narrow dusty streets, to find that it was just a tawdry, mud coloured town, like every other city of the

Sketch 9 Kut to Shahroban. Chapters IX and X

East. A ruder shock awaited us. Baghdad had occupied our thoughts for so long that it had not occurred to anyone that this would not be our final objective. The brigade marched right through the city, and out of the northern gate. A bivouac site had been allotted to us in a clearing among the date groves at Moazim. As we marched into camp, we were informed that the brigade would continue the trek at dawn next morning.

Chapter X
Battle of The Jebel Hamrin, 25 March 1917

The suddenness of our move onwards was a great disappointment to officers and men alike. Officers' mess stores were completely exhausted, while the men had run out of those two absolute necessities of the sepoy, namely, sugar and milk. Cigarettes had become a priceless possession, and we were reduced to those of Arab manufacture, which certainly made up in strength for what they lacked in tobacco. However, the men were wonderfully cheerful about it all, especially when the reason for our advance was explained to them.

The capture of Baghdad by the British had severed the communications of the Turkish force that was opposing the Russians in Persia. This Turkish force was composed of the 2nd and 6th Divisions, the former of which, it will be remembered, had been our opponents in the Battle of Beit Aeissa.

As its former line of retreat was now cut, this force commenced to fall back along the Khanikin road, followed by the Russians, and was making for Kizil Robat, and the fords over the Diala River nearby (Sketch No. 9). Having crossed the Diala, the two divisions could still escape to the north, by a mountainous road via Kirkuk, to Mosul. It was with the object of seizing these fords, and so cutting their only remaining line of retreat, that our brigade was sent so hurriedly forward.

Our column was to consist of the 8th and 9th Brigades, with attached cavalry and guns, the whole under the command of General Keary. The 8th Brigade were already at Bakuba, on the Diala River.

On 18 March we left Baghdad, and trekked to Khan Beni Saad. This was the most unpleasant of our marches since leaving Shumran. Owing to delays in drawing rations, the brigade did not set out until 1 p.m. It was intensely hot, and along all the dreary 19 miles, the most desolate country imaginable was passed through. The dry, sun-baked plain. was devoid of any sort of vegetation, dead or alive, and the monotony of it was only broken by the occasional banks of dry, and long since disused canals. The country round Baghdad is, if possible, drearier than that round Kut. In the latter area the soil is cultivatable, and is usually covered with a kind of dwarf scrub; round Baghdad it becomes a hard marl plain, on which nothing will grow, and which even the nomadic Arab tribes leave severely alone.

On arrival at bivouacs that night, the only water available was from an exceptionally filthy nala; and a gale, which sprung up in the middle of the night, added to the general discomfort.

Next day the brigade marched to bivouacs on the right bank of the Diala, opposite Bakuba. That night we crossed the river by moonlight, on a rickety pontoon bridge, to bivouacs in an orange grove near the town.

Bakuba was by far the prettiest spot we ever saw in Mesopotamia. A quaint little Arab town, it nestled in the midst of most luxuriant orange and date gardens, on the banks of the river. The following day is to be remembered as one of our most pleasant experiences during the war. It was a complete rest, and the men lazed the day through in the shade of the orange trees, with boots off to ease their aching feet. The oranges of Bakuba are famous, and the memory of them lingers in one's mind like that of the Baghdad lettuces.

It was with the greatest regret that we continued the trek on the morning of 21 March, just as the first tints of dawn were appearing above the distant Persian hills.

We bivouacked that night at Abu Jisra, the 8th Brigade, with which we had caught up at Bakuba, being still one day ahead.

At Abu Jisra, Keary's column first came in contact with the enemy – a flank guard covering their eventual retreat across the Diala. A small body of these had taken up a position between Abu Jisra and Shahroban, and orders came for the 9th Brigade to do an encircling movement round their left flank, before dawn on 22 March. These orders were cancelled during the night, and next day the enemy evacuated their position, and retired on to the Jebel Hamrin.

Shahroban, which thus fell into our hands, was a pleasant little town, encircled in palm groves. The whole country, indeed, after Bakuba, had taken on a different aspect. Intersected by numerous water-cuts, it appeared green and prosperous, and, except for the lack of trees, resembled nothing so much as a fertile plain in India.

The 8th Brigade followed up the Turks when they retired, and took up an outpost position between Shahroban and the Jebel Hamrin.

On the 23rd, our brigade marched from Abu Jisra, and bivouacked just west of Shahroban, arriving there at about midday. Below is a table of marches from Shumram to Shahroban, showing halts, and distances covered:-

Date	Halting Place	Miles
8 March	Imam Mahdi	15
12 March	Ash	18
13 March	Azizieh	20
14 March	Zeur	15
15 March	Boston	16
16 March	Diala	12
17 March	Baghdad	14
18 March	Khan Beni Saad	19
19 March	Bakuba	17
21 March	Abu Jisra	16
23 March	Shahroban	9
Eleven Marches		**171**
Average March		**15.5**

We had just got comfortably settled into camp at Shahroban, when news came that the brigade would march that night, and attack the enemy at dawn.

Before describing the action at Jebel Hamrin, it will be necessary to give the reader a short account of the situation, and the surrounding country. From Shahroban, the ground undulated gently downward to the Beled Ruz and Haruntyah Canals, two deep water-cuts some 30 feet across (Sketch No. 10). From here it stretched in a level, grassy plain to the Jebel Hamrin, a large, rugged range of hills, some 300 feet higher than the surrounding plain, stony, and without shape or form.

The scheme was for the 8th Brigade to attack the enemy frontally, while the 9th Brigade, having entered the hills clear of the enemy's left flank by a night march, was to envelop it simultaneously with the frontal attack. The enemy, according to our intelligence (chiefly derived from deserters' stories) were 2,000 strong, with six guns.

Before dusk on 23 March, bivouacs were struck, and the regiment marched through Shahroban (where Lieutenant Rigg and two platoons of B Company were left as garrison), and assembled at the brigade rendezvous about a mile east of the town.

Here the whole brigade remained until 11 p.m., when the march commenced. C Company, under Captain Pegg, was detailed as escort to guns, much to the disgust of the latter, who thought he would miss the fight. The column was extremely long, containing, besides the 9th Brigade, a bridging-train, and much artillery.

It was one of the most tedious night marches that the regiment ever made, and was interspersed with long halts, during which it was almost impossible to keep awake. A hitherto unknown water-cut was met, which had to be bridged before the column could pass. The result was that, after some six hours marching and halts, dawn found us only about four or five miles from our starting point. We had arrived at the canals at the point where Campbell's Bridge was afterwards constructed. (Sketch No. 10)

These canals were artificial, and the earth thrown out in their construction formed banks along the edge, from two to eight feet high.

As day broke the predicament that the column was in became apparent, and everyone hastily took cover along the banks of the canal. It is doubtful if this deceived the Turk; anyhow he refrained from shelling us that day, which was spent by us in furtively watching him over the banks of the canal, and in making up for arrears in sleep. During the day the sappers were busy constructing the two bridges across the Haruniyah and Beled Ruz Canals, (shown in Sketch No. 10).

Even if the Turks could not see the infantry, these working parties must have been very obvious. Towards evening there was great activity on the part of the enemy in the Jebel Hamrin. Large bodies of men could be seen moving about in the hills, the general direction of their movements being, apparently, towards our front.

It was certainly plain to everyone in the 9th Brigade that there were more than 2,000 enemy there, and, as events afterwards proved, there were not only 6,000 rifles against us, but also 24 guns. This was not all. The 8th Brigade was held up, so that the frontal attack could not take place. The scheme, therefore, had now resolved itself into this – that the 9th Brigade, numbering well under 2,000 rifles, was to butt its head into an unknown, and particularly rugged range of hills, unsupported by guns, there to meet a concealed enemy, numbering about 6,000 rifles and 24 guns, and possessing a perfect knowledge of the ground.

All this, of course, was not known at the time. The number of the enemy was uncertain. It was not anticipated that our guns would be totally unable to distinguish our troops from those of the enemy in the hills, and that they therefore would have to remain silent. The facts have been laid bare beforehand so that the reader can better understand the sad story which follows.

The movement of the enemy in the hills, who were obviously reinforcing their flank opposite us, was reported to Brigade

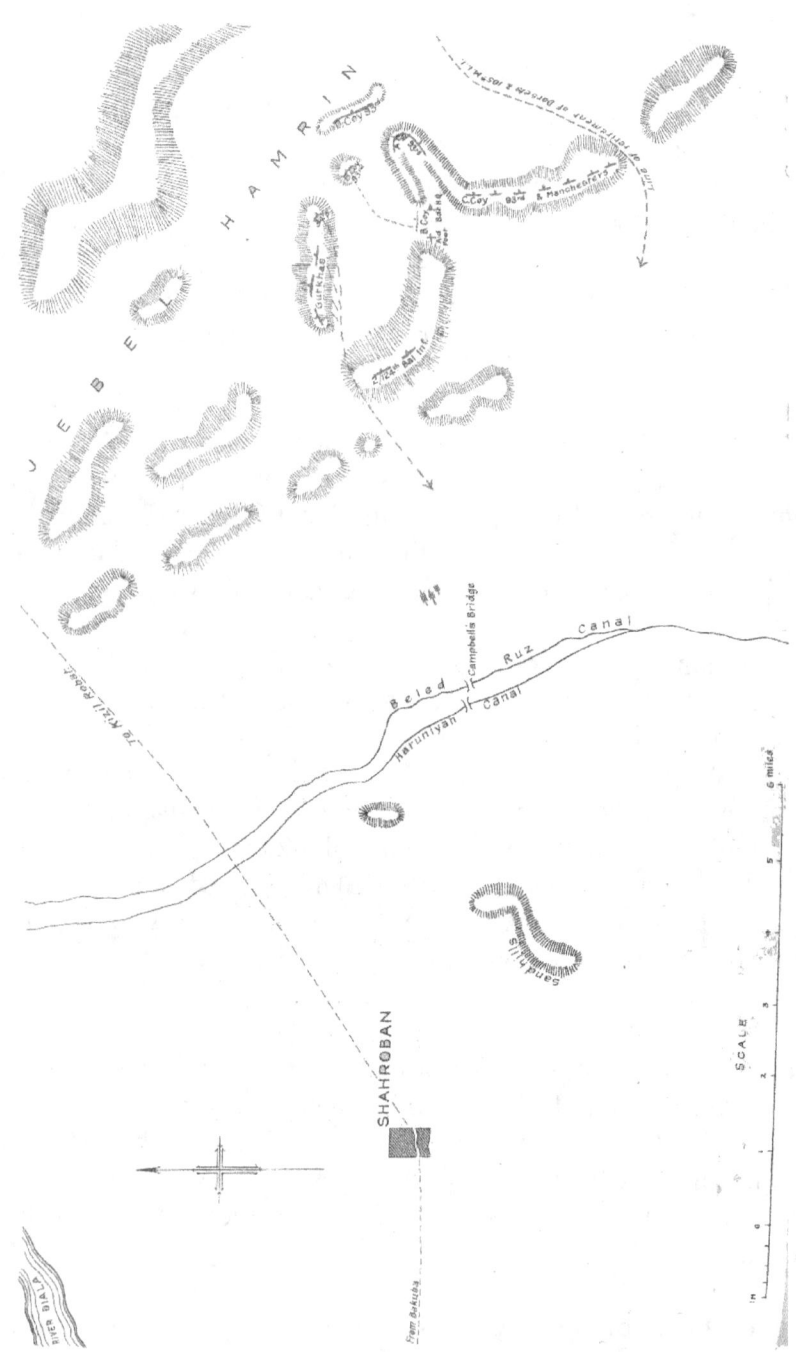

Sketch 10 The Jebel Hamrin. Chapter X

Headquarters, and from brigade to the column. General Campbell, also, hearing that the 8th Brigade could not now cooperate, protested against the task allotted him, and it is believed that the column commander protested to G.H.Q. Be that as it may, orders came that it had to be done; and at 9.15 p.m. that night (24 March) the brigade moved.

People had plenty of food for thought during the ensuing march. Hopes of success did not appear bright. Everyone knew that there were more enemy than they had been told; and that their arrival next morning would hardly come as a surprise, as they had seen the enemy reinforcing their line opposite; moreover, half the attacking troops (the 8th Brigade) would not participate, and, after 24 years of fighting in the plains, the 9th Brigade were to be launched into hill warfare, about which very few of them remembered anything – a type, moreover, more formidable than that on the North-West Frontier, where the enemy possess neither bombs, machine guns, shrapnel, or discipline.

Our only chance appeared to lie in the hope that the enemy were thoroughly underfed, and demoralised by our capture of Baghdad. It was disappointing next morning when the first prisoners turned out to be the fat, smiling, well-clothed, Anatolian Turk, of the 2nd Division, that we had met at Beit Aeissa.

At 1 a.m. the brigade had reached the beginning of the foothills, and formed a square, with the transport animals in the centre. C.O.s went to Brigade Headquarters to have the scheme explained to them. At 4.30 a.m. the brigade would continue the advance in diamond formation as follows – Dorsets leading battalion, 105th Mahrattas right, 1-1st Gurkhas left, and the 93rd in the rear. After entering the hills, the brigade would left-turn, the 1-1st Gurkhas thereby becoming the leading, Dorsets the right, and the 93rd the left, battalion. This latter movement, however, never took place. Battalions themselves were to advance in diamond formation of companies in fours. After orders were received, we composed ourselves for slumber such as our premonition of disaster, and the chilly wind, would allow.

The more one reflects on our position that night, the more it will appear one which courted calamity. The whole brigade lay there in a compact square, with some two or three hundred animals in the centre. It was within a half-mile of the enemy's picquets, and about 10 miles from its base. An enterprising attack during the night would have driven it into the wildest confusion. It may be that the enemy picquets were asleep, or it may be that it was their plan to lure us into the hills; whatever it was, the night passed uneventfully, and at dawn we advanced.

In a short time, the brigade was swallowed up in the hills. At first little opposition was met with; but gradually the enemy's resistance began to stiffen, until finally the brigade was firmly wedged into the hills, and surrounded on all sides except the one by which it had entered.

Companies of the 93rd were sent to different points to strengthen the line, including C Company, under Captain Pegg, which rejoined the regiment during the morning. The final position of units was as shown in Sketch No. 10. The situation gradually began to take on a very ominous aspect. Enemy machine guns were placed in prepared positions, which were impossible to spot, and their fire laced the top of the ridges on which we sat. Their guns, too, knowing exactly where our troops were, and the configuration of the ground, made things decidedly unpleasant.

Apart from this, the intricate nature of the hills enabled the enemy gradually to assemble men under cover for surprise counter-attacks. It soon became apparent that this was what they were doing, and that our position by night would be extremely precarious, for, not only could they attack frontally, but, under cover of darkness, they could descend to the plain, and cut our line of retreat, unseen by our guns behind.

It was not only frontal fire that had to be contended with. As our line took the form of a semi-circle, one was always liable to be hit in the back by "overs" from some other part of the line, and casualties were experienced among people sitting in what were, apparently, the most secure positions. Our artillery sitting some two miles back could not distinguish friend from foe, and our artillery screens, which drew a hail of bullets when hoisted, had to be abandoned. The Turk had it all his own way. Judging rightly that the depressions concealed from his view would hold our reserves, he plastered them with a fairly steady stream of shrapnel. True, the guns were of small calibre, but nevertheless they made things decidedly unpleasant.

The Dorsets and 105th Mahrattas were gradually pressed back from their advanced positions, and things were looking so black that General Campbell decided to retire while there was still light to do so. Accordingly, he gave orders that the 93rd, Manchesters, and 124th Baluchis (the last two regiments of the 8th Brigade having just arrived in support) would remain as rearguard, and that the other units would retire forthwith.

On receipt of orders the remaining units went as fast as their legs would carry them for Campbell's Bridge, while B and D Companies of the 93rd withdrew from their advanced positions to the general line.

As soon as the rest of the brigade was well away, the rearguard regiments also commenced to retire. This was no easy matter, as we were too closely engaged with the enemy. As long as our force remained in the hills it did not present unsurmountable difficulties, but, directly the last lines got into the plain, further halting was suicidal, as the enemy, being still in the hills, had cover, while our men had none.

Now commenced one of the most unpleasant experiences imaginable, i.e., that of retiring across a level plain, by day, with rifles, machine guns, and shrapnel, lacing into our backs. The pace was that of the slowest man, that is, the wounded, and it is a wonder how anyone came through unscathed. All around the spits of dust proclaimed the striking bullets, while shrapnel, fired obliquely, searched up and down the retiring lines. Luckily, the enemy, fearing our guns, did not follow far into the open, and, when we had put some 2,000 yards between ourselves and them, they gave up firing in order to loot the killed and wounded.

Many were the pitiful scenes which must have been enacted in the hills after our departure. The wounded had to be carried all the way to Campbell's Bridge on stretchers. Those men wounded after the last relay of stretcher-bearers had left, had to shift for themselves. Men too badly wounded to walk, had to be left behind, and these were practically all murdered, probably by the Arab hangers-on, who always follow a Turkish army in the field, much as vultures follow a convoy of animals across the desert.

Our casualties by now had become very heavy. Major Haughton was wounded through the calf, Lieutenants Oatway and Lalor had both been wounded in the leg earlier in the day, and had to be evacuated. During the retirement, Captain Pegg was wounded both in the leg and the chest, while Lieutenant Scott was hit in the head. Lieutenant Pearson was last seen giving water to a wounded soldier in the hills. He was never seen, or heard of again.

Of the Indian officers, Subadar Major Madat Khan, Subadar Wariam Singh, and Jemadar Maghar Singh were killed, while Subadars Balaka Singh, Basant Singh, and Jemadar Mahomed Sayed, were wounded. Our total casualties were 153, or 30 percent of the numbers engaged.

Thus ended one of the most disastrous actions the regiment went through, and it was not until 18 months later that we got our revenge on the Turk.

In a successful attack, the opportunities for the display of personal bravery are rare; in a reverse, they are common. When one's mind is fired with the elation of certain success, it is not hard to be brave;

when it is cowed by the knowledge of disaster, and sacrifices made in vain, the impulse of bravery does not readily come to the fore. On this day many very heroic deeds were performed; but as awards are not given to defeated troops, not a single decoration was received by the 9th Brigade for that day.

As at Beit Aeissa, Major Morgan (now C.O. for the third time) was congratulated, both by the Divisional and Brigade Commanders, for the steadiness of the regiment during the retirement.

That night the remnants of the brigade bivouacked at Campbell's Bridge, and next day returned to Shahroban.

On 27 March, a wild report arrived that the enemy were congregating on our right flank, and the 93rd was sent off once more in the direction of Campbell's Bridge. The enemy turned out to be a flock of sheep, but nevertheless an outpost line was put out facing south-east, with the left near Campbell's Bridge, and here we remained until 2 April.

On 31 March, after a few reconnaissances to find if the Jebel Hamrin was still occupied, the 8th Brigade pushed through unopposed to Kizil Robat, and joined hands with the advanced troops of the Russians, the Turk, in the meanwhile, having retired across the Diala.

Now that connection with the Risdinny was established, orders came for Keary's column to return to Baghdad. Accordingly, on 3 April, the brigade marched to Abu Jisra. As the weather was now very warm, we marched from here onwards by night, usually starting at 1 a.m.

From Abu Jisra the stages were Bakuba, Cassell's Post, Baghdad, the second one of 24 miles, being a particularly trying march.

Chapter XI
The Euphrates Treks

We left Cassell's Post at 2 a.m. on 6 April, and, after a ten-mile march, arrived outside Baghdad at daybreak.

Approached from the east, Baghdad does not present such a pleasing picture as from the south. It appears to consist of little more than an expanse of evil rubbish heaps and ruins, in varying degrees of decay. The city has been decimated so many times by siege, sickness, and massacre, that its shrinkages and expansions are marked by a fringe of ruins, which get more and more decrepit as they go eastwards, until they merge into the desert itself. The environs, however, as seen in the light of early dawn, are distinctly striking. To the south stretch the date gardens we had passed through on our first entry, while, to the north, the early light shows up the golden domes and minarets of Khazimain and Moazim.

Our second march through Baghdad gave us a much better impression of the town than our first. Instead of keeping to the main road, we went through the bazaars – those quaint covered-in bazaars, peculiar to the Near East – and thence across the river. The shops were gradually filling up with the goods that had been hidden by their owners when the British first arrived in Baghdad. The anticipation of being able to spend money again was very pleasant to officers and men alike.

Our destination was Khazimain, where B and D Companies relieved the Black Watch, of the 7th Division, on picquet duties from the river bank north of Khazimain, to Khazimain railway station, and thence along the railway embankment to Zobeida's Tomb. From here the 1-1st Gurkhas carried on the line to the Iron Bridge. The remaining two companies, with Battalion Headquarters, camped in a palm grove between Khazimain and Baghdad.

After a few days of much-needed rest, orders came at 1 a.m. on 9 April for a flying column of 350 rifles (100 rifles Dorsets and 250 rifles 93rd) to proceed forthwith to Mufraz on the Euphrates, some 25 miles away. The column was accompanied by a section of guns, and a section of No. 112 C.F.A., the whole under the command of Major Morgan.

Having only a few hours' notice, and these being hours of darkness, the column assembled at the rendezvous, and set off, leaving orders for the transport to follow with an escort of 50 rifles under Captain Haycraft.

The country between Baghdad and the Euphrates is perhaps the most desolate of any in a country which breathes desolation. In the shimmering haze of a midday sun its dreariness is indescribable. For the most part hard and gravelly, it is completely devoid of any vegetation, and abounds with mounds covering the remains of old and forgotten cities and towns. Indeed, from Babylon to Nineveh, the most common objects lying around are fragments of old and sun-dried brick and pottery, to which the familiar green and blue glaze still adheres, all remnants of the days when this was a fertile and luxuriant land.

Let us return, however, to our tale. Having crossed the Iron Bridge across the Sakhlawiyah (afterwards called Khwarr) Canal, the column proceeded into the blue for about 10 miles, where, finding some wells, Major Morgan decided to halt, and await the transport. The latter, which assembled at the Iron Bridge at 1 p.m., joined the column at dusk, accompanied by Captain Marshall, 37th Dogras, as Political Officer. We all became very much attached to Marshall during the next few months, when we saw quite a lot of him. Poor fellow, he was murdered by fanatics at Nejf, some 10 months later.

The object of the column was to find out if all was well with a detachment of the 27th Punjabis at Mufraz, with which communication had been cut, and around which the Arabs were known to be restless. After halting the night at the wells, the march was continued before dawn, and the column arrived at Mufraz at about 9 a.m. to find the detachment under Major Vernon flourishing, and quite unaware of the concern they had aroused.

Next afternoon we commenced the return march at 2 p.m., and, after halting the night by the wells, arrived at Baghdad on 12 April, and resumed our outpost line through Khazimain.

On 13 April, Colonel Haughton rejoined, though somewhat prematurely as it afterwards turned out.

A few days afterwards our camp was moved to another palm grove, and, while here, the leave season to India opened, Captain Hodson and Lieutenant Smith being the first to go. At this time, also, Captain Coningham from the 96th Berar Infantry, and 2nd Lieutenant McClenaghan from the 129th Baluchis, joined as reinforcements.

Towards the end of April, the necessity for another movable column arose. Arabs from the direction of Mahmudiyah had cut the embankments of the Decauville railway to the Euphrates, in order to let the water of the Sakhlawiyah Marsh through to the south; they were also holding up, and robbing, the pilgrim caravans on the road to Kerbela. Consequently, it was decided to send down a column of one battalion of infantry, two guns, some cavalry, sappers, and a wireless section, the whole under the command of Colonel Powell, R.A. The infantry battalion was the 93rd, and in order to enable us to go, the Dorsets, who were standing by for column duties, relieved us in the outpost line.

Our camp at Khazimain was left in charge of Lieutenant Oatway, who, together with Lieutenant Scott, had just returned after their wounds at the Jebel Hamrin, and on 30 April, the regiment paraded at 6 a.m. and proceeded to the column rendezvous, near the Iron Bridge, in a blinding dust storm.

That night, after dark, the column marched, the immediate objective being Khan Azad, a deserted police post which was supposed to be the headquarters of the Arab robbers. After proceeding about three-quarters of the way, we halted until 3 a.m. Resuming the march, the column got quite close to the Khan by dawn. As soon as it was visible through the growing light, the 93rd deployed, and made for it, while the cavalry tried to encircle it. Our guns, which opened fire simultaneously, gave warning of our approach too soon, and the cavalry, whose detour was too wide, were unable to surround the Arabs, who were well mounted, and fled helter-skelter. The 93rd nearly distinguished itself by opening rapid fire on Colonel Powell and a few orderlies, who careered off madly in pursuit, but were luckily checked in time.

After a few hours halt at Khan Azad, the column pushed on to Mahmudiyah, leaving some sappers to make a somewhat ineffectual attempt to demolish the Khan.

On the way to Mahmudiyah, we shelled some encampments belonging to the robbers; but beyond collecting a lot of sheep and cattle, and killing some Arab women and children by shellfire (the men having all fled) little retribution was exacted. The column stayed that night at Mahmudiyah, and, leaving C Company under Captain Coningham there, with the guns and cavalry, proceeded to Iskandariyah next day.

Both Mahmudiyah and Iskandariyah are ordinary desert Arab towns, and their inhabitants, either through fear, or thankfulness at being temporarily rid of the robbers, received us with the fluttering of many white flags. Neither place had any particular charm, but our final destination, Museyib, to which the column marched after leaving Iskandariyah, was otherwise.

Museyib stands at the point where the pilgrim road to Kerbela, perhaps the second greatest place of Mohamedan pilgrimage, crosses the Euphrates. Surrounded by palm groves and cultivation (thanks very largely to Willcocks' Barrage, which raises the river level to that of the surrounding country) it is a picturesque town, in whose quaint bazaars all types of Arabs can be met.

Here can be seen the degenerate, pale-faced town-dweller rubbing shoulders with the fierce, hawk-eyed Arab of the desert, and merchandise exposed for sale, ranging from garden produce, to murderous knives and bandoliers, and intricately woven saddlery. We were the first British to arrive in Museyib, and our appearance caused considerable curiosity, and the display of many white flags.

The column camped in a palm grove close to the town, and the time passed pleasantly and uneventfully, except for the rifle thieves, who, around Museyib, were very active. The fact that the camp was nearly surrounded by trees was to their advantage, and a cordon of sentries did not prevent them stealing one rifle.

On 7 May, to his own and everyone else's disgust, orders came for Major Morgan to return to Baghdad, and officiate as G.S.O.1, 3rd Division.

A few weeks afterwards, the column commenced the return march to Baghdad, leaving B and D Companies, under Captain Haycraft, behind as a detachment. The day being cool, it was decided to march to Mahmudiyah in one stage. As soon as Iskandariyah was left well behind, it turned excessively hot, and the regiment had a trying march before it reached Mahmudiyah.

Picking up C Company and the guns, the march was continued, and Baghdad reached on 27 May. On arrival, Lieutenant Trevelyan proceeded on leave to India, Lieutenant Rigg officiating as adjutant. Two new I.A.R. officers awaited us at Baghdad, namely, Lieutenants Lee-Warner and Rowbotham, also Lieutenant Lalor, who had returned after his wound at the Jebel Hamrin. Our camp had also been changed. The mess had moved to the last house on the left-hand side of the road, where the tramlines leave the outskirts of Baghdad for Khazimain, while the men camped in the first date grove on the right-hand side of the road after leaving Baghdad.

These quarters, which we occupied during the worst of the hot weather, when not on trek to the Euphrates, were by far the best we ever had during the war. The officers had a house to live in, while the men had E.P. tents on the very banks of the river.

The only bugbear to our life at this time was the convoy to Nukta, a pestilential spot halfway between Baghdad and Feluja. These convoys carried rations to the 7th Brigade, who were at the latter place. They were escorted by 50 rifles, under a British officer, as far as Nukta, 25 miles away, where the convoy was taken over by a similar escort of the 7th Brigade, and our escort returned home. Owing to the intense heat at this period, these convoys left Baghdad in the evening, and marched all night.

On 4 June, B and D Companies, which had stayed at Museyib on detachment duty, returned. After staying at Museyib a few days, the detachment had moved down to the Hindiyah barrage, some seven miles downstream, where it camped at the junction of the Hillah Canal with the Euphrates. On 2 June, the detachment was relieved by the 27th Punjabis, and, picking up Lieutenant Scott, who was assisting the Local Supply Officer at Museyib, returned by easy stages to Baghdad.

For some time, Colonel Haughton had been troubled by the old wounds he had received at Beit Aeissa, until finally, on the advice of a specialist, he left the regiment, and was invalided out of the country. At this time, also, Lieutenant Oatway went on leave to India.

On 22 June, Major Morgan was relieved on the divisional staff by Captain Coningham, and returned to command the regiment for the fourth time.

Rumours had long been busy about an expedition against the Turks at Ramadi, their lowest point on the Euphrates, some 30 miles west of Feluja, and on 6 July, during early morning parade, orders came for the 1-1st Gurkhas and 93rd to march and join the 7th Brigade next day. Leaving Lieutenant McClenaghan in charge of the camp, the regiment marched at 4 p.m.

Taken all round, this was the most wonderful achievement in

marching that the regiment ever did. For several days previously it had been getting steadily hotter, so that all through the operations the temperature in the shade averaged 120 degrees by day. We had, moreover, received several new drafts, who had had no practice in marching – indeed the whole regiment had led a very sedentary life for over a month.

We crossed the Iron Bridge at dusk, and, picking up the 1-1st Gurkhas, continued the march to the first halting place – Nukta – 25 miles away. After a longish halt in the middle of the night, to allow some carts to be extricated from the difficulties they had got into, Nukta was finally reached many hours after dawn. After a day in the scorching sun, with nothing but brackish water to drink, the march was continued at dusk, and the column arrived at Feluja, 18 miles away, at 3 a.m. Up to this point only two men of the 93rd had fallen out.

At Feluja we heard the details of the scheme (Sketch No. 11). The 1-1st Gurkhas were to garrison Feluja, and the entrance of the Sakhlawiyah Canal, in the absence of the 7th Brigade. The latter, with the 93rd attached, were to march that night to Sinn al Zibban. The 93rd would garrison both Sinn al Zibban and Mahdi, and the 7th Brigade would then march through and attack Ramadi.

Accordingly, that night the 7th Brigade and 93rd assembled at the rendezvous on the right bank of the Euphrates, and marched at 11 p.m. We were rear battalion. The road was very rough, and many carts overturned in the thick sand, with the result that the rearguard did not arrive at Sinn al Zibban until several hours after daybreak.

The 7th Brigade was to continue the march that night (10 July) and attack the Turks at Ramadi the following day; but, before this could be done, the defile at Mahdi had to be secured. For this purpose, B and D Companies, under Captain Haycraft and Lieutenant Lalor, preceded by some cavalry, marched from Sinn al Zabban at 4.30 p.m. The Turkish post at Mahdi fled, and the defile was occupied without opposition by dusk. Shortly after, the column, under the command of

Colonel Haldane, 7th Gurkhas (General Davidson, G.O.C. 7th Brigade, being on leave) marched through.

The details of the failure of the first Battle of Ramadi, on 11 July, do not concern this narrative. Suffice is it to say that the 7th Brigade were set an impossible task, which no troops could have accomplished in that heat. Suffering agonies of thirst, they had to lie out all day, with the temperature at 124 degrees in the shade. It was decided to withdraw in the evening.

Though expected at Madhi, they did not arrive that night, but withdrew to some shade on the banks of the river until the early morning of 13 July, when the retirement commenced. As soon as this started, the Turks and Arabs followed them up, until they arrived within the shelter of the 93rd picquets at Mahdi. The Turks made several attempts to advance on these picquets, but they were beaten off, and by midday fire ceased.

That evening, the retirement continued to Sinn al Zibban, our half-battalion, with two guns and two armoured cars, forming the rearguard. As soon as the column got clear, and the main guard were moving, the rear party under Lieutenant Lalor left the hills, and went as fast as their legs could carry them. Luckily, no enemy followed them up from behind, but the retirement was along the bank of, and parallel to, the river, and a continuous fire was kept up by Arabs hidden in the long grass on the other bank. This fire, mostly from antique firearms, though very inaccurate, was quite disconcerting, as the range was under two hundred yards. They succeeded in killing one, and wounding two men of B Company.

By the time we were clear of the hills, it was dusk. The remainder of the column had disappeared into the blue, and it was 9 p.m. before the rearguard companies rejoined Battalion Headquarters at Sinn al Zibban. The 7th Brigade returned to Feluja next day, and, after being relieved by the 6th Jats, the 93rd followed them a few days later.

Before leaving Sinn al Zibban, we had the satisfaction of seeing the villages, from which we had been sniped during the retirement from Mahdi, effectively shelled.

The regiment marched to Feluja on the morning of 16 July, and continued the march to Nukta the same evening, covering this last 18 miles in 6 hours, and in all 28 miles that day. Next night, we marched to a camp on the edge of the Sakhlawiyah Marsh, near the Iron Bridge, halting for the day, and going on to Baghdad the same evening.

Our return to Baghdad that night was celebrated in a fitting manner, the simultaneous arrival of Lieutenant Hodson from leave being an additional cause for jubilation. Later General Edwardes (in the absence of General Keary on leave) personally expressed his appreciation of what the 93rd had done. The regiment had covered 126 miles in eight marches, of which two had amounted to 50 miles, through the most intense heat of the year, and during the march only four men had fallen out.

That was our last visit to the Euphrates, and it is probable that no one, who had experienced the terrible dreariness of that sun-baked track to Nukta, was sorry. During the heat of June and July, it had fallen to our lot to do more marching than, probably, any regiment in Mesopotamia. These marches had, of necessity, been mostly by night. Their memory is not, perhaps, so unpleasant as that of the marches before Dujailah or the Jebel Hamrin, where the mind was filled with forebodings of the day to follow; but night-marching of any kind is a most wearisome occupation. The days, too, offered no relief. During the Ramadi operations, tentage was carried to the scale of one 160lb tent for 20 men – a covering which offers little protection when the thermometer stands at over 120 degrees in the shade.

The regiment stayed in the camp near Baghdad until 2 August, when it was ordered to move up to Khazimain, where the remainder of the brigade was encamped. The mess was in an old serai, while the men lived in the same palm grove which had been left when the regiment marched on the column to Museyib.

Our quarters in the serai were quite comfortable, and the view of an evening from the roof was very fine. As the sun fell behind the waters of the marsh to the west, making a black silhouette of the mysterious temple of Akarkuf, the golden mosque behind took on a warmer and richer hue. Indeed, the whole city appeared more beautiful at this hour. The muddy colour of the river, and the drab houses which fronted it, became tinged with delicate shades of rose and gold by the evening light, and one became imbued with something of the mystery of this ancient city, once so fine and now so sordid.

Lieutenant Smith had already returned from leave, and soon after Lieutenant Trevelyan also arrived, while Captain Coningham rejoined from the staff. We lost Lieutenant Coffey, however, who went sick at this period, and returned to the depot in India. A Company was taken over by Lieutenant Trevelyan, C by Captain Coningham, and Lieutenant Rigg remained as adjutant. Pending the arrival of two more Lewis Guns per company, teams were being trained ready for them, while tongues wagged merrily over rumours of coming strife, and offensives in the cold weather.

On 15 August, General Campbell addressed the officers before relinquishing command of the brigade. He had been with us for 18 months, and his perpetual cheeriness and bluster had endeared him to all. Many were the times in later days when we wished he was back with us. There were not many dry eyes at the end of the interview, including those of the general himself.

Captain Buckland, the brigade major, had also left, and the whole outlook seemed changed. There is nothing so disheartening to a soldier on service as the change of a popular commander. It is impossible for a newcomer to realise the trials and hardships of the past. In a regiment which has been long on service, many little points of discipline are relaxed.

There is less precision in the handling of arms; equipment and

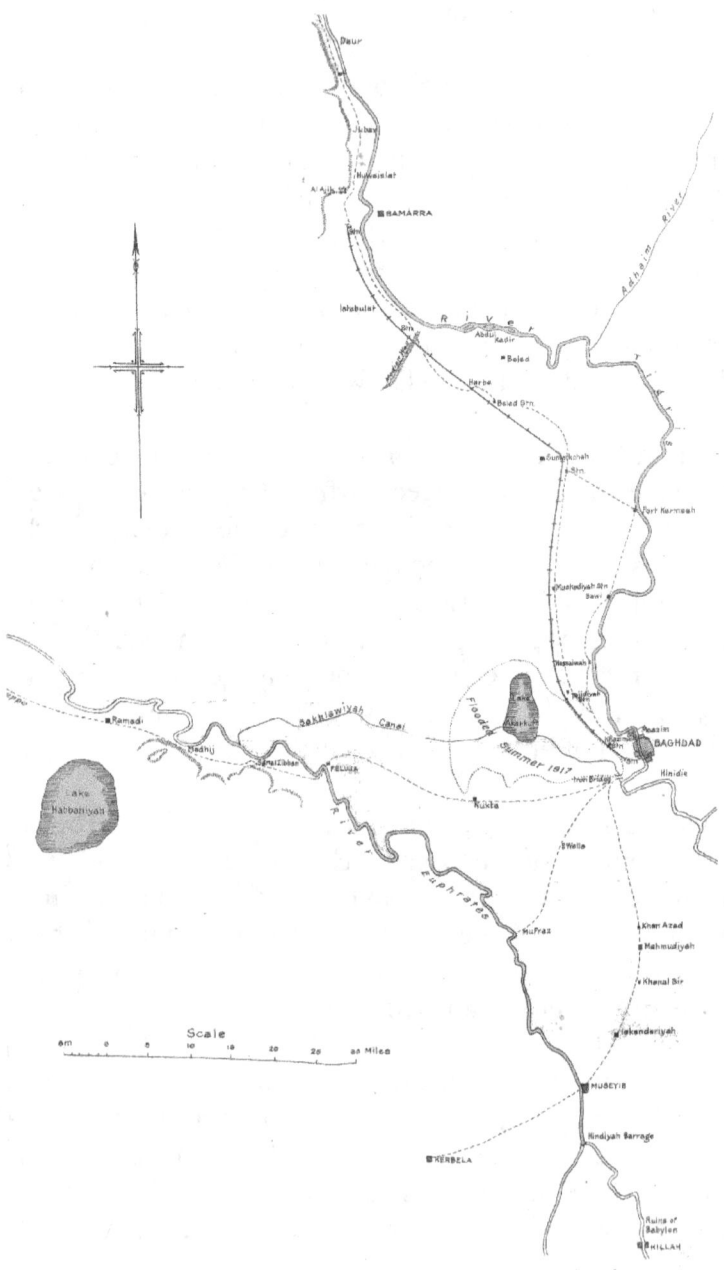

Sketch 11 Samarra, Baghdad, and the Euphrates.
Chapters XI and XII

clothing are not so spick and span; it is realised that the best march discipline is that which makes a man arrive at the other end, i.e., the wish to do so, and not necessarily that which keeps him correctly aligned in fours. These things, however, may appear due to inefficiency to a man fresh from the drill-grounds of India.

On 19 August, a wire informed us that Major A. Bredin, hitherto second in command of the 72nd Punjabis, which regiment had been in India since the beginning of the war, had been appointed commandant.

So once again Major Morgan would revert to "second fiddle." He had brought us out of action as C.O. in the Battle of Beit Aeissa. He had commanded us in the Battle of the Apex. He had brought us out of action as C.O. after the operations in the Mahomed Abdul Hassan Bend, and again at the Jebel Hamrin. Moreover, G.H.Q. Mesopotamia applied for him to be left in command. Yet Simla thought otherwise.

Before leaving, General Campbell sent us a private letter, which read as follows:-

> On handing over the command of the 9th Brigade, the G.O.C. wishes to place on record his appreciation of the work done by the 93rd Burma Infantry. The regiment joined the brigade in January, 1916, since when it has taken its full share of the fighting, privations of heat and cold, and heavy marching, which has fallen to the lot of the brigade. It is regretted that their casualties in British and Indian ranks have been heavy. The good spirit pervading all ranks, and their loyal cooperation in the brigade, are much appreciated; the credit for this is due to Colonel Morgan, and his officers, British and Indian.
>
> The G.O.C. wishes all ranks farewell, and all good fortune in the future.

The new brigadier was General Luard, with him came [A. F.] Harper, 84th Punjabis, as brigade major.

At this time a shifting of brigades took place, and the 9th Brigade was ordered to Beled, in place of the 8th Brigade, who were to move on to Istabulat. The 7th Division was to remain at Samarra. The 93rd was ordered to march ahead, and report on the route, the remainder of the brigade following later.

Chapter XII
Beled and Samarra

With many regrets, the regiment left Khazimain on the evening of 22 August, halting the first night at Hassaiwah. The next stage took us to Bawi, and the third to Fort Kermeah. From Fort Kermeah we struck inland to Samaikchah, and the next march took us to Beled.

All these marches were done by night, but the stages were easy; and, at the first three halts, the bathing in the Tigris was delightful.

Beled was a pestilential spot. The camp was near the railway station, and laid out so that the length was parallel to the prevailing wind. To add to the discomforts, all mounted troops, such as artillery, were camped at the windward end. The result was a veritable sea of dust, and sand-devils, which careered through the camp, creating havoc in their wake. Washing water was scarce, and had to be drawn from wells, the river being too far off to be of any use. In fact, the only charm of Beled lay in the Arab town, some four miles away, the gardens of which teemed with black partridge.

Beled was the headquarters of the 9th Brigade for some three months, during which the time alternated between intensive training, digging, and marching to Istabulat and back again.

Colonel Bredin joined the regiment on 28 August, and, soon after, General Keary sent us the following letter on relinquishing command of the 3rd Division:-

> During the time this regiment has been under my command, I have noted with great pleasure the fine fighting qualities and soldierly bearing it has displayed. Having been acquainted with the regiment since its formation, and having the personal acquaintance of many of its officers, British and Indian, it has given me more than ordinary gratification to observe its good work.

> Though I have had to regret the loss of two old friends in Lieutenant Colonels Stevens and Whitehead, it has been some consolation to know they died as they would have wished, as brave soldiers at the head of their regiment. I tender my thanks to all ranks for their discipline, good conduct, and fine work at all times. I wish all ranks, and especially old friends of the regiment, farewell, and the best of good fortune at all times.

General Keary's successor was General Hoskings, who had been transferred from East Africa.

It was decided to make a third line of defence at Beled, the front lines being at Samarra and Istabulat, respectively. For this purpose, the regiment had to march out an hour before dawn, and do night operations for the two or three miles to the digging site. Then, after three to four hours' digging, open warfare practices were indulged in on the way home. Instruction, imparted in such concentrated doses, did not, one imagines, materially improve our efficiency.

While at Beled, honours for the spring campaign were published. Major Morgan received a long overdue D.S.O., Subadar Lachhman Singh the I.O.M., Havildars Bhan Singh, Sahib Singh, and Naik Feroz Khan, the I.D.S.M., while Naik Bahadur Khan received the Russian decoration of Saint Georges, 2nd Class. Shortly afterwards Jamadar Sheikh Abdulla also received the I.D.S.M.

Presently digging camps were established, one at Abdul Kadir on the river bank, and one at Harbe. The latter was a disagreeable place owing to the lack of water, but the proximity of the river for bathing and fishing, and of Beled town for shooting, made Abdul Kadir the most popular camp in the brigade area.

We spent a week at Harbe, after which the Dorsets relieved us there. No sooner had we arrived back at Beled, than orders came for the 93rd to march that night to Istabulat, some 18 miles away. A Turkish force from Tekrit was demonstrating in front of Samarra. The 8th

Brigade was marching to Samarra, and the 93rd was to escort the 4th Brigade R.F.A. as far as Istabulat, and there take over the 8th Brigade camp.

The regiment marched at 10 p.m., the rearguard arriving at Istabulat camp as late as 10 a.m. next morning, owing to the difficulty of getting the heavy artillery wagons through the thick sand.

Istabulat was a delightful camp compared to Beled. Lying just south of the old Roman town, it was on the banks of the Tigris, the water of which was here as clear as crystal.

Most of the enemy in front of Samarra having turned out to be an enormous flock of sheep, the 8th Brigade returned to Istabulat in a few days, and the 93rd, unhampered by guns, covered the 18 miles back to Beled in six hours.

Shortly after our return to Beled, we went to the other digging camp at Abdul Kadir, on the river bank. Officers and men alike had been looking forward to the sojourn in this camp as a relief after the monotonous sand of Beled. But on the first day a dust storm of such magnitude blew that we were unable to leave our tents, and on the next day we were ordered to return to Beled.

Things were again getting troublesome up Samarra way, and the 9th Brigade marched that night for Istabulat, leaving the 93rd to occupy the camp at Beled. Two days later we followed the brigade, two platoons of B Company, under Captain Haycraft, having previously been sent by train to garrison Istabulat railway station.

Though we did not know it at the time, this was our final goodbye to Beled. It had been decided to mop up the Turks at Tekrit. Accordingly, the 7th Division, with 8th Brigade attached, moved out from Samarra, the remainder of the 9th Brigade at Istabulat replacing them in the Samarra area.

Our march to Istabulat was unpleasant, as it was intensely cold, and there was a long halt in the middle of the night, near the Median Wall, to extricate some Ford vans, which had got stuck in the thick sand.

We remained two days at Istabulat, and at 9 p.m. on 4 November, resumed our march northwards, accompanied by the 72nd Howitzer Battery, and a battery of field guns. A guide was to meet the regiment at Samarra, with instructions to put us on the straight road to the east of the railway station, but he took us to a bivouac ground on the west instead. Here another guide found us, who took us to the empty headquarters of the 19th Brigade, and eventually we marched through the wire at Al Ajik, and on to Jabur, arriving there at 7 a.m.

After a halt of two hours, the regiment marched on past C.P. (the advanced base and refilling point for these operations) to the old enemy trenches at Daur, from which the 7th Division had evicted the Turks. We arrived there at 3 p.m., having covered 32 miles in one march. Even then, many men went off to the river, five miles away, to bathe.

The regiment remained in this bivouac for several unpleasant days. The nights were cold, and, as all the transport was required for rations, we had none for blankets; the days were hot, and the flies worse than anything imaginable. Orders were received to make a tactical reconnaissance of the old Turkish position, and 'to fill in the trenches.' After much hopeless spade work, it was found that we were meant to fill them in on the map!

While the regiment was here, Captain Trevelyan went to C.P. as post-commandant, taking A Company with him. Later on the whole regiment concentrated there, where it remained as rearguard, while the 7th Division marched through on their way back to Samarra. On the evening of 10 November, we proceeded to Huwaislat, and rejoined the 9th Brigade, returning from there to a bivouac area west of Samarra station.

Orders were now issued for the 3rd Division to relieve the 7th Division, in the Samarra area. The 7th Brigade were to occupy the position on the left bank, and the 9th and 8th Brigades from right to left, respectively, on the right bank. The 9th Brigade camp was just below Salabiyah and Al Ajik, and our regiment relieved, and occupied the camp of the 92nd Punjabis. On relief the 7th Division marched down stream.

The 3rd Division stayed at Samarra for nearly five months, during which life was quite uneventful, and in many ways very pleasant. Although there were no enemy within 80 miles or so, every night a company and a half had to sleep in the trenches, while by day a company from the brigade went out as a covering party. Training was very intense, and became monotonous, but was often relieved by quite strenuous, and often amusing, brigade field-days.

A most cheerful Christmas week compensated us for the miserable one we had spent the year before; but just at its conclusion, to the intense regret of everyone, officers and men alike, Major Morgan left to command a new unit in India. He ultimately raised the 3-70th Burma Rifles, at Meiktila.

At this time Lieutenant Oatway, who had been ill after his leave in India, rejoined; also Lieutenant Smith, who had been attached to the S. and T. Corps for some time. January also saw the return of Captain Pegg, who had been wounded at the Jebel Hamrin. For a short time, he took over adjutancy from Lieutenant Lalor, who had relieved Lieutenant Rigg, but soon relinquished it in order to command D Company.

Some sporting events at this time added interest to life. The regiment was unsuccessful in the cross-country race, but won the Samarra football tournament fairly easily.

Early in the year, the 7th Division had left for Palestine, and although everyone expected that our division would follow them, hope was lost as the time passed, and no orders came.

In March, however, it became evident that something was in the wind. Feverish efforts were being made with the continuation of the railway towards Tekrit, and the 3rd Division was more or less under orders to move at short notice. Betting was about equal as to whether we would move up or down stream, and it was not until two days before marching that it was definitely known that we were going south.

On 12 March, the 9th Brigade was relieved by a brigade of the 17th Division, a new division which had been forming downstream, and marched to a camp near Samarra railway station. Here we were informed that our destination was Palestine.

The trek downstream commenced on 18 March, the first two stages being done by night, in order to escape observation by enemy aircraft. The stages were Istabulat, Beled, Sumaikchah, Mashadiyah, Khazimain, Baghdad.

We marched through Baghdad on the 24th, to a camp near the new railway station at Hinaidie, and after a day spent in sorting kits, entrained for Kut on the anniversary of the Battle of Jebel Hamrin. Kut, with its stations, wharves, and warehouses, was unrecognisable, but the old trenches in the Mahomed Abdul Hassan Bend had changed but little. That evening the regiment embarked on the *P92*, a palace compared with the P boats of old, and in the morning steamed through the land so full of memories of the past.

Next morning the regiment disembarked at Amara, and marched to the rest camp. Here intensive training commenced again, and it was quite a relief when we entrained for Nahr Umr.

At Nahr Umr, a new wharf which had sprung into existence north of Basra, most of the 3rd Division was collected, and regiments were being taken away as shipping became available. Ours was almost the last to leave.

On 3 May, we embarked on the SS *Barala* and sailed to the Bar, where, at the point we had passed nearly 30 months before, we transhipped to the Orient boat, SS *Ormonde*, a magnificent Australian liner.

Our departure from Mesopotamia was hardly as anticipated. For two years the occasion had been longed for, talked of, and dreamt of, and one had expected it to occur with an orgy of celebration. When it did come, it passed over much as a matter of course. So much for our dreams.

The 47th Sikhs shared the boat, and such was its size that even the sepoy had no complaint as to overcrowding. Every person present will, undoubtedly, look back on this voyage as one of the most pleasant they have experienced. Inter-regimental sports were arranged with the 47th Sikhs, for long our rivals on the hockey field, and on 15 May we arrived at Suez.

PART IV

PALESTINE

Chapter XIII
Hot Weather, 1918

The regiment disembarked from the SS *Ormonde* on 16 May, having received instructions to entrain that evening for Moascar, where the 3rd Division was concentrating.

Beyond the addition of a few dilapidated reed huts, Moascar had changed but little; we camped on the identical spot where we had been some three years before.

As is inevitable when a regiment moves from one Force to another, this was a busy time for the adjutant and quartermaster – Lieutenant Lalor and Captain Hodson. The Egyptian Expeditionary Force had hitherto been almost entirely composed of British troops, and the administrative services had different methods from those of Mesopotamia. This called for a lot of heavy work from the regimental staff, to bring things into line with the new conditions.

We now heard for the first time the reason of our move from Mesopotamia. The German offensive in France had necessitated the transfer of several British divisions to that front, and the 3rd and 7th Divisions had come to take their place in Palestine.

While the C.O. and his staff wrestled with the apparently endless office work, companies occupied their time with intensive training, though no one had the vaguest idea as to what kind of warfare the regiment would shortly be engaged in, as this varied on the Palestine front from trench warfare in the coastal sector, to hill warfare in the country west of the Jordan. It was interesting, however, to parade over ground which brought back memories of past experiences, though sad to think of the changes in the regiment that had since occurred.

On arrival at Moascar, we were informed, much to our disgust, that a company would have to be sent away to a new unit – the 2-153rd Infantry – which was just being raised. In spite of our protests, a complete Sikh company was insisted on, and Colonel Bredin decided to send away A Company, under Captain Trevelyan and Lieutenant Smith. It was annoying to find out afterwards, that none of the other three regiments who sent men to this unit had detailed complete companies.

Short leave to Cairo opened while the regiment was at Moascar, and most British officers, and a large number of men, were able to get away. Captain Haycraft was detailed at this time to take up an appointment as instructor in the Indian School at Zeitun, and left before the move from Moascar took place.

On 30 May, the regiment commenced the journey to Palestine. The first march was to El Fardan, the second to Kantara, and thence by rail to Ludd, where we arrived on 1 June. Kantara was hardly recognisable. Our little, old, perimeter trenches were lost in a forest of tents, sheds, workshops, and railway yards. Only the Quarantine House, police post, and mosque, stood to remind us of what it had looked like three years before.

At Ludd, orders arrived for A Company to proceed to join the 2-153rd Infantry at Sarafend, and they marched straight from the station to join that unit.

The brigade, which we had now rejoined, was camped at Haditha, some four miles north-east of Ludd (Sketch No. 12), and three weeks of intensive training followed. The camp was at the foot of the hills, and was suitable for practising mountain warfare, and every effort was made to get the men fit for the ensuing operations. The 9th Brigade was then used as Corps Troops, and was actually the only reserve in the country.

At this time the men's bandolier equipment was changed to the old

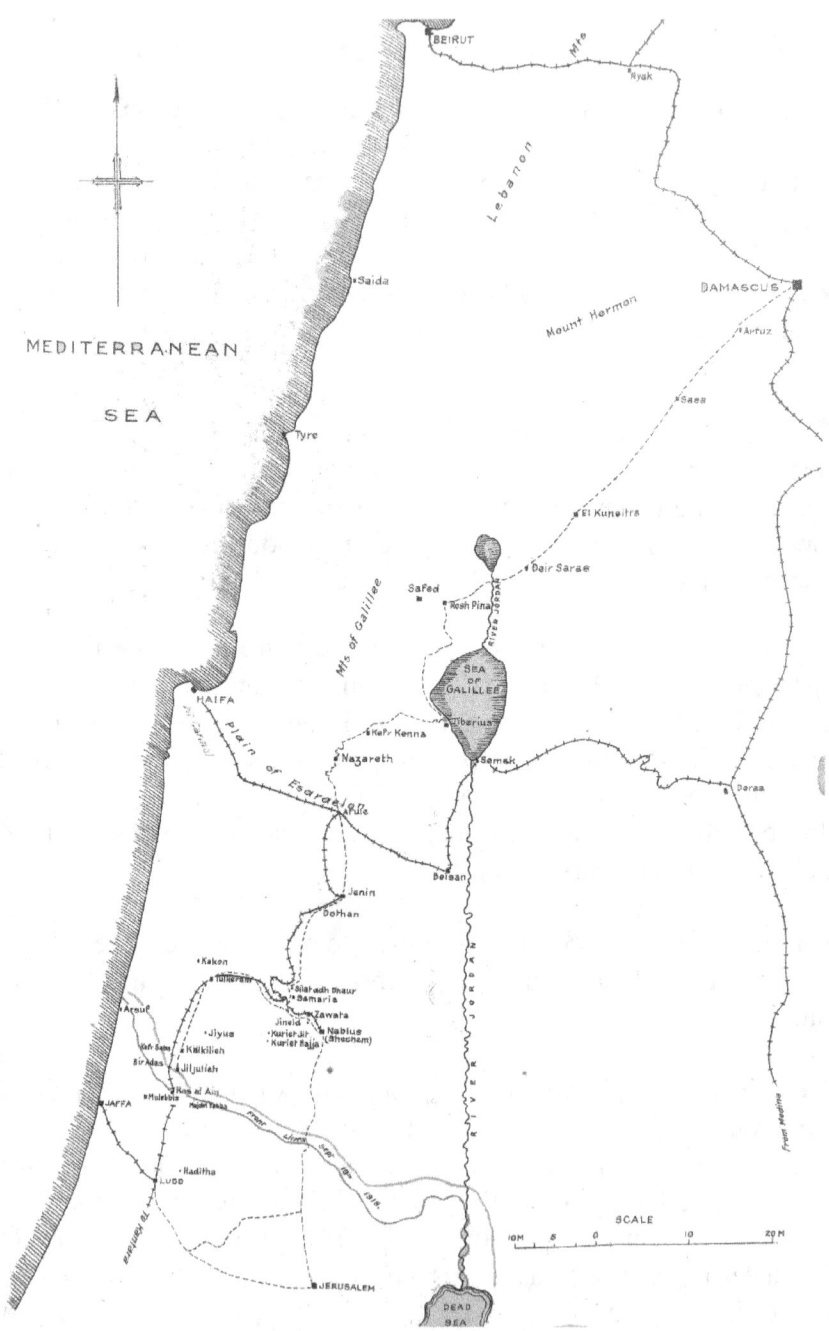

Sketch 12 Palestine and Syria. Chapters XIII, XIV and XV

infantry equipment, with leather pouches and braces, a more unserviceable equipment than which it would be hard to find. The pouches were bulky and uncomfortable, and shed their contents whenever their owner moved out of a walk.

At midday on 22 June, orders were received to move that night. The brigade marched to Mezeireh, arriving at midnight, and bivouacking until dawn. Next morning, advanced parties went on to examine the line to be taken over, and, at night, the regiment relieved the 1-11th Londons, of the 54th Division, in the right sub-section of the Mejdel Yabba position. C, B, and D Companies held the line, from right to left, under Major Coningham, Lieutenant Oatway, and Captain Pegg respectively, while the new A Company, which was formed from one platoon of Sikhs from B Company, and two platoons of P.M.s from C and D Companies, and in which there was no British officer, remained in reserve.

The enemy line was quite far away, and the only trouble was caused by Ikbar, a deserted village close to our picquets. On the night of 26 June, a patrol under Jemadar Bhan Singh met with strong opposition there, but the enemy left next day, when a patrol under Lieutenant Scott found it empty.

On 4 July, the regiment was relieved by the 105th Mahrattas, and went to brigade reserve in the Boundary Wadi. On the night of 13 July, there was heavy shelling. The Turks intended to attack at Rafat and Ras al Ain in order to assist an attack by the Germans in the Jordan Valley, but the demonstration was a poor one.

Four days later, the regiment was relieved by the 124th Baluchis, and went to rest bivouacs in the almond groves south of Mulebbis. On this day Colonel Bredin, who had been suffering in health for some time, left the regiment. Shortly after, Major W. H. Ralston, 47th Sikhs, assumed officiating command.

Strenuous precautions were at this time being taken against gas, and all the men were passed through a gas chamber at Mulebbis.

Towards the end of July, the 3rd Division moved towards the coast, and the 9th Brigade, being on the left of the division, took over the section of the line between Mukhmar and Boche Woods (see Sketch No. 13). The 93rd, as brigade reserve, went to bivouacs at White Ruin Garden, near the Auja River.

While here, Captain Haycraft rejoined from Zeitun, where he had been replaced by Captain Pegg, much to the latter's disgust, and resumed command of B Company.

During the night of 31 August, the 93rd relieved the Dorsets in the line, where the time passed pleasantly enough. In spite of constant patrolling by night, a Turk was never seen during the whole of our stay in the line, while the proximity of the Auja River, a mysterious stream which springs from the ground near Ras al Ain, added greatly to our comfort.

During the night of 7 September, the regiment was relieved by the 91st Punjabis, and marched to Greek Farm, some six miles back, arriving after midnight. Fever, caught from the rank vegetation round Mukhmar Wood, now became rather prevalent, and both Lieutenants Campbell and Grundy, who had just joined, were transferred to C.F.A.

So passed the hot weather of 1918 – more pleasant than either of the two preceding ones. The climate of Palestine is infinitely preferable to that of Mesopotamia, while the country, with its rolling downs and vineyards, is more pleasing to the eye than the glaring monotony of the deserts in the "Land of the Two Rivers."

The morale of the Turk after his heavy defeats, both in Mesopotamia and Palestine, was very low at this time. Our patrols held complete mastery of no-man's land by night, and an "affair of patrols" was a rare occurrence indeed.

Although facing the enemy, the conditions contained little of the unpleasantness of real trench warfare, owing to the distance between the two lines, and the lack of initiative of the Turk. Indeed, until the offensive, which opened on 19 September, the regiment did not suffer a single casualty in Palestine.

Chapter XIV
The Battle of Brown Hill and After

From the thousand little signs inevitable on such occasions, it was now apparent that operations on a large scale were in course of preparation, and it was no great surprise to us at Greek Farm, when the brigade was practised in attacking a system of trenches resembling those of the enemy at Brown Hill. These parades usually commenced at about midnight, and, after an attack at dawn, were carried well on into the morning.

After an interval of intensive training at Greek Farm, we again took over the same section of the line from the 7th Brigade, the Dorsets and 105th Mahrattas being in the front line, and the 93rd in reserve at White Ruin Garden.

Here details of the forthcoming offensive gradually came to hand, equipment, bombs, et cetera, were overhauled, and movements of large bodies of troops, and guns, took place by night, from east to west, behind us.

The Turkish trenches extended in a continuous line from the sea coast, to near Bir Adas village, the country in this sector being open and undulating. From Bir Adas, a clear expanse of undefended level plain stretched to the trenches of the Railway, and Jiljuliyah Redoubts. From here, eastwards, the hills commenced, and the defensive system of necessity resolved itself into a line of isolated strongpoints.

Our troops were disposed as follows. The 7th Division held the line from the sea coast to the Hadrah Road (Sketch No. 13), from where the 3rd Division continued the line to opposite Jiljuliyah. To the east of this, the hill sector was held by the 10th, 53rd, 54th, 60th, and 75th Divisions.

The idea of the operations was as follows:

On the night of 17/18 September, a feint attack, to distract the enemy's attention, was to be made between Jiljuliyah and the Jordan, while the next night the main attack was to take place between Juljuliyah and the sea. In order to assist in this main attack, the 60th and 75th Divisions were brought from their section of the line in the hills, and were concentrated between the 3rd and 7th Divisions. It was the rumbling of their transport and guns that we heard by night behind us.

The pivot of this attack was the strongly entrenched position on Brown Hill, and the Railway and Juljuliyah Redoubts, the task of taking which was entrusted to the 3rd Division. To the left of the latter the 75th and 7th Divisions carried on the attack to the sea coast, with the 60th Division, in reserve.

Having broken the crust of the enemy's resistance, the three attacking divisions were to wheel to the right, using the 3rd Division as a pivot, until they faced east, and were then to advance into the hills on to the Jerusalem – Nablus road (Sketch No. 12). Meanwhile, three cavalry divisions would sweep northwards along the sea coast, and cut the enemy's communications further up.

The front of the 3rd Division was from the Hadrah Road on the west to Juljuliyah on the east (see Sketch No. 13), and the scheme for attack was as follows. The 9th Brigade was to attack from the Hadrah Road to point 247 exclusive, the second objective being Hill 283, and point G28 inclusive. The 7th Brigade was to attack on the right of the 9th Brigade, its objectives being the point 247, and Fir Hill up to G25. Meanwhile the 8th Brigade was to demonstrate in front of the Railway and Jiljuliyah Redoubts, but was not to close with the enemy until the 7th and 9th Brigades had gained their objectives.

In the brigade scheme, the 105th Mahrattas and Dorsets were in front, from right to left, respectively. They were to capture the enemy's system as far as G9, when the 93rd (behind the 105th Mahrattas) and the 1-1st Gurkhas (behind the Dorsets) were to leapfrog, and take Hill 283 and G28. From here the brigade would wheel to the right, the final objective for 19 September being the village of Jiyus, in the hills.

Zero hour was at 4.30 a.m. on the 19th. The brigade, which was to be extended on markers in front of Boche Wood beforehand, would advance at zero minus 3 (i.e. 4.27 a.m.). The bombardment would commence at zero, and, the pace of the infantry being calculated at 100 yards a minute, the time for lifting from trench to trench was minutely laid down.

Major Coningham, as second in command, and Lieutenant Campbell, who had just returned from C.F.A., and was surplus to our strength, were left with the 1st Line Transport. Companies therefore were commanded as follows: A Company by Lieutenant Oatway, B by Captain Haycraft, C by Lieutenant Scott, and D by Lieutenant McClenaghan. Lieutenants Lalor and Rigg accompanied Battalion Headquarters, the former as adjutant, and the latter as intelligence officer.

After a somewhat cheerless meal at 12.30 a.m., the regiment paraded, and marched to the point of assembly at Boche Wood. Here guides met companies, and took them to their platoon markers, which had previously been posted by Lieutenant Rigg. B and D Companies were in front, from right to left, respectively, with A and C Companies behind.

Some activity on the part of the enemy machine guns as we got on to our markers did not tend to make the prospect more cheerful, as we feared it meant that they knew we were coming. Gradually the minutes ticked themselves away, and at 4.27 a.m. the advance commenced. Giving us three minutes to clear the rise in front, our guns started at zero.

The din was terrific, and the rain of shells of all calibres, from field guns to 8-inch howitzers, screeched a few feet above our heads. Only those who have stood in front of a line of guns spitting fire can appreciate the ear-splitting noise they make.

From this point any exact or methodical account of the attack is impossible. Though the first glimmer of dawn appeared when the advance commenced, and it gradually became more and more light, the fumes and smoke of the barrage obscured everything in a hazy mist. The leading companies had, perhaps, passed halfway across no-man's land before the enemy's counter-barrage commenced, but the din was so terrific that only their 5.9 inch crumps were discernible above the rest. The lesser noise of shrapnel was lost in the unceasing roar.

The bearing of the advance was 50 degrees, but it was quite impossible to use a compass, and keep moving at the same time. The stars, too, were hidden in the smoke. Consequently, direction was somewhat lost.

All that is certain, is that B Company, with A Company behind, went too much to the right, and, bumping up against point 247 in front of the 7th Brigade, whose objective it was, left inclined. At this time D Company also edged off to the right, and the two companies crossed in front of G2, without seeing each other.

From this point onwards, D Company was on the right, and B on the left. The advance continued without opposition. Batches of prisoners in twenties, thirties, and fifties, were collected, and left behind, and guns ranging from 77mm to 5.9 inch, still smoking from the barrage they had put up, were passed by uncounted.

The enemy's second line at G28 was crossed without opposition, and, wheeling to the right, the leading companies halted, and reformed in some gardens overlooking the low ground north of Kalkiliah.

Our casualties had been extraordinarily light. Lieutenant Oatway had been wounded in the leg by shrapnel early in the attack, and Lieutenant Rigg had met sundry bits of a Turkish bomb near G2, where he had attempted to tackle a machine gun nest nearly single-handed. This, indeed, was the only attempt at opposition put up by the Turks during the attack.

The direction of fire in front of divisions on our left, showed that they had broken through equally successfully, and, as soon as the 1-1st Gurkhas had drawn level, the advance eastwards, preceded by patrols, was continued.

On our right, the 7th and 8th Brigades could be seen advancing, and at about 8 a.m. we crossed the Kalkiliah – Tulkeram road. Communication with Brigade Headquarters being now completely lost, a halt was made on some rising ground a mile east of the road. This halt continued until 2 p.m., by which time the 1st Line Transport, under Lieutenant Rowbotham, had joined up. There was still no sign of the brigade staff, and, mainly through the exhortations of Colonel Ralston, assembled C.O.s decided to push on to Jiyus independently. The advance was approved of by General Luard, who arrived soon after, and was continued well into the hills, units marching more or less independently.

The 105th Mahrattas, with A and C Companies of the 93rd under Lieutenant Scott who had lost connection with the remainder of the battalion, went via a nala on the right, and arrived at Jiyus before dark. On arrival at the village, Lieutenant Scott captured a large batch of prisoners, including two German officers.

The remainder of the battalion, with the 1-1st Gurkhas and the Dorsets, were caught in a defile on the left by some enemy machine guns, which made the nala impassable until dark. After much consultation, no definite orders being obtainable from the brigade, it was decided to bivouac for the night where we were, though some anxiety was felt about Lieutenant Scott, and his two companies, whose whereabouts was unknown.

Next morning, 20 September, the brigade marched at 5 a.m., with the 93rd as advanced guard, the objective being Kefr Kaddum.

The 105th Mahrattas, and Lieutenant Scott's two companies, joined the column at Jiyus, after which the brigade filed into the Wadi Sir – a precipitous nala with high hills on either side. The progress of the brigade being extraordinarily slow, Colonel Ralston, as O.C. advanced guard, decided to push on to Baka, a village on the crest of a hill, 1,516 feet high. We arrived at Baka at 11 a.m., and halted until 1 p.m., awaiting the arrival of the brigade.

From Baka the country as far as Kuriet Jit was visible like an open map before us. The winding ribbon of the road from Azzun could be seen crowded with enemy transport, trekking northwards. Taking advantage of the opportunity given, the regiment pushed on to Kuriet Hajja as soon as permission could be obtained. Arriving there Colonel Ralston gave the order to cut the road, although this was not our objective.

Led by D Company, under Lieutenant McClenaghan, who was Q.C. advanced party, the appearance of the 93rd on the road caused consternation and havoc amongst the Turks. Those that could, whipped up their tired animals, and escaped northwards; but these were few, and soon the road was a congested muddle of transport vehicles, and guns of all descriptions. Over 20 guns of large calibre, we were afterwards told by the divisional commander, were caught by our cutting the road.

Soon after this, some alarmist messages told us that the enemy were attacking, and that we were likely to be cut off. These messages had no foundation in fact, but were sufficiently disconcerting to cause us to move our position back some 300 yards, to the high ground overlooking the road, east of Kuriet Hajja. The regiment's bag of prisoners that day was 250, including many Germans. Next day, we found the name of a regiment in another brigade, which had arrived on the scene after us, imprinted on all the guns that we had captured.

That day's march had been very trying. The tortuous route had been along a mountain track, over very hilly country. We were lucky to have a more or less peaceful night in which to recover.

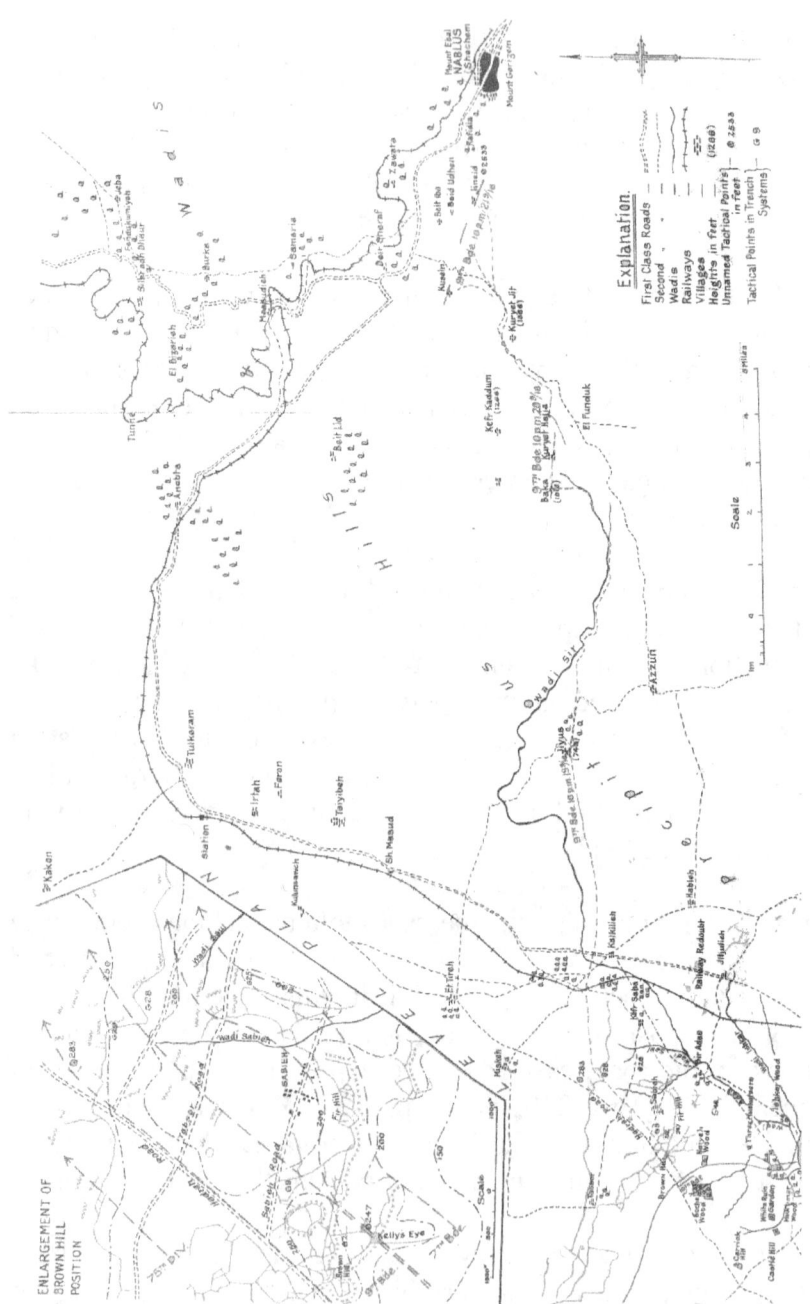

Sketch 13 Brown Hill to Nablus. Chapters XIII, XIV and XV

Next morning, 21 September, the advance continued at 5 a.m., the brigade's objective being the Nablus – Samaria road, and our regimental objective being the village of Jineid, and Hill 2533. Turkish transport and guns littered the road. We collected all the animals we could, and, for the next few days, the regiment was followed by nearly 100 animals, ponies and donkeys, carrying packs, and other irksome but necessary impedimenta.

While passing through Kuriet Jit, General Hoskings, the divisional commander, rode up to Colonel Ralston, and congratulated him warmly on the achievements of the regiment the previous day.

Jineid and Hill 2533 were two towering prominences near Mount Gerizem, and overlooked the Nablus – Samaria road. They were about ½ mile apart, and separated by a slight col, while, from between the two, a deep gully, with spurs on either side, wended its way towards the line of our approach. C and D Companies, under Major Coningham, worked up the spur to Jineid, and A Company up that to Hill 2533.

A few Turks could be seen in or about Jineid, but these quickly evacuated the village on the approach of C and D Companies, and retired on to Hill 2533, up the spur to which A Company was slowly climbing. Arriving at Jineid, Colonel Ralston ordered D Company to take Hill 2533, on which the enemy had machine guns, but, before D Company could arrive, A Company, under Lieutenant Scott, had cleared the hill.

The regiment remained at Jineid for the rest of that day and night, during which our cavalry cleared Nablus of the enemy. Once we had arrived there, and recovered breath sufficiently to take stock of our surroundings, the view from Jineid was delightful. Some thousand feet below us, the white road, gleaming like a silver streak in the sunshine, wound northwards to Samaria. To the east, appeared the tiled houses and gardens, on the outskirts of Nablus, while, all around, lay the tumbled brown hills of Palestine.

During the morning of 22 September, we evacuated Jineid, and went to bivouacs near the village of Beit Iba, remaining there two days, and putting out outposts by night round Beit Udhen.

On 24 September, the brigade marched to Messudieh. Here the other three regiments bivouacked, while the 93rd marched on to Silat adh Dhaur, where the most delightful bivouacs were obtained in a fig garden on the side of a hill. We all expected to continue the trek northwards after a few days' rest, but, to our disgust, on the evening of the 28th, orders came to march forthwith back to Messudieh. Arriving after dark, the regiment bivouacked at Messudieh, and next day the brigade marched to Kakon, north-west of Tulkeram, leaving Lieutenant Scott, with A Company, as guard over the tunnel near Anebta.

Next day, the brigade returned to bivouacs at Jiljuliyah, thereby closing our active participation in the operations. These, indeed, after the first few days, had become remote from the sphere of the slow-moving infantry, and had given the cavalry their first real chance in the war.

This was the last battle that the regiment participated in during the war, if, indeed, one can grace it by the name of battle. There was little shell fire, and no rifle or machine gun fire to be faced. That hateful crack of the bullet, or swish of a traversing machine gun, or thudding of bombs, was absent, but no one could have wished the war to wind up in any other manner. We may not have had to fight very hard for our revenge, but it was nonetheless complete, and the memory of Dujailah, Beit Aeissa, and the Jebel Hamrin, may fairly be said to have been wiped out.

Our casualties in the whole operations amounted to under a hundred, or 15 percent of the numbers engaged, but these figures were the highest in the brigade. There was not a single casualty among the Indian officers.

Chapter XV
Damascus

The 9th Brigade, with the 8th Brigade alongside, remained in bivouacs at Jiljuliyah for nearly four weeks. Though comfortable enough in many ways, it was a pestilential camp, and fevers, and stomach troubles, were very prevalent. Lieutenant Campbell, however, was the only officer transferred to C.F.A.

While here, Lieutenant Oatway rejoined, and took over A Company, which had returned from its guardianship of the tunnel. Lieutenant Lewis, who had hitherto been with cavalry, also joined as a reinforcement.

While at Jiljuliyah, Captain Bostock left the Brigade staff to take up a higher appointment. He had been staff captain for over two years, and his departure was greatly regretted by everyone.

On 16 October, the rewards for the operations were published. Lieutenant McClenaghan, and Subadar Harnam Singh, received the M.C., and Havildar Mahomed Sowar the I.O.M.

We had been expecting for some time to move northwards, and, towards the end of the month, it was definitely known that our destination was to be Damascus.

On the 27th, the 9th Brigade marched to Tulkeram. Owing partly to excessive packs (complete winter clothing having to be carried on the man) and partly to many men not having recovered from illnesses contracted at Jiljuliyah, more men fell out on this march than on any other during the war.

Next day, the brigade moved to Zowata, where they remained until 1 November. This march was also a very trying one. We left Tulkeram at 3 a.m., and did not arrive at our destination until after 11 a.m. The road was hemmed in by high hills, and there was no breeze to carry away the choking dust. At Zowata news of the long expected armistice with Turkey was received. Considering that this was the realisation of our hopes for many years, it is surprising how little enthusiasm it evoked.

From Zowata, all marches commenced between 1 a.m. and 3 a.m., in order to avoid the heat of the day. The chief places of interest on the road were Nablus (the biblical Shechem), Samaria, Nazareth (a most picturesque village perched on the heights around the Plain of Armageddon, and through which we marched at dawn), Kefr Kenna (known in connection with the early days of Christ), and Tiberius on the Sea of Galilee. This lake of crystal clear water is a beautiful sight nestling among the rugged brown hills which surround it. We had a whole day here to laze through, with our boots off, and the bathing was delightful.

The following table shows the halts and distances covered. It will be noted that the stages were, for the most part, fairly easy ones:-

Date	**Destination**	**Miles**
27 October	Tulkeram	13
30 October	Zowata	17
1 November	Silat adh Dhaur	9
2 November	Jenin	16
3 November	Afule	12
4 November	Kefr Kenna	13
5 November	Tibermws	13
7 November	Rosh Pina	16
8 November	Deir es Saras	13
9 November	El Kuneitra	10
10 November	Sasa	19
12 November	Artus	12
13 November	Damascus	8
Thirteen marches		**171**
Average March		**13.2**

At Rosh Pina, sad news arrived of the death of Major Alves. He had commanded the depot in India for over three years, but there were few officers left in the battalion who knew him.

On 8 November, the brigade crossed the Jordan by the "Bridge of Jacob's Daughters." The desert winds had now become bitterly cold, and everyone was thankful for the warm kit that they carried with them. After the bitter experience of turning out at 1 a.m. at Deir es Saras to march to Kuneitra, we trekked henceforth by daylight. The face of the country had now completely changed. It was bleak and uninteresting, and covered with enormous boulders of volcanic formation.

After Kuneitra, we were supposed to halt at Nahr Mughaniyah, but owing to a lack of topographical skill on the part of our staff captain, we overshot this place, and arrived at Sasa, - having done two stages in one day. As this gave us a day's halt at Sasa, few people were sorry that the mistake had been made.

The rain, which had been threatening for some time, broke on our arrival at Artuz, and a miserable night was spent under our insufficient covering.

On 13 November, the brigade arrived at Damascus. The rain ceased at daybreak, and it was a cold, crisp, morning, while Mount Hermon, to our left, had taken on its first covering of snow during the night.

After the dreariness of the country beyond the Jordan, Damascus appeared as an oasis in the desert. It is surrounded by the most beautiful wooded gardens, which are watered by the famous Pharphar and Abana Rivers, and for which the bare slopes of Hermon form a perfect background.

Though we had entertained hopes of obtaining billets in Damascus, our expectations were not realised. Instead, we were camped at El Mezze, just outside the gardens to the west of the city.

The 9th Brigade spent just a year at Damascus, which passed without incident, and which, but for the climate, would have been very pleasant. The discomfort of the incessant rain during the cold weather was aggravated by the gales, which swept from the Mountains of Lebanon down on to the Damascus Plain. Even after the rains had ceased, these winds continued right into the autumn, causing, as soon as the ground was dry enough, the most distressing dust-storms.

The city of Damascus is both picturesque and interesting, and the bazaars – larger and better stocked than those at Baghdad – gladdened the hearts of the sepoys. For the officers, there were trips to Beirut and Baalbek, both of which were within easy distance by rail.

Captain Pegg, and Lieutenant Rigg, rejoined the regiment soon after its arrival at Damascus, but this period saw the departure of most of our Indian Army Reserve Officers. In the spring of 1919, Captain Hodson, and Lieutenants Scott, Rowbotham, and Lee-Warner, left for demobilisation.

While not wishing to minimise the devoted services rendered to the regiment by all Indian Army Reserve Officers, it is necessary to single out Captain Hodson for our special thanks. He served with the regiment for 4½ years, during 3½ of which he was quartermaster. Though continually the martyr of a tyrannous stomach, he only went sick on two occasions, and then only for a few days at a time. His tact and business experience made him an ideal man for the job of dealing with the cantankerous breed of underlings found in the Ordnance, and S. and T. Corps; while his cheerfulness and lack of expectation of respect for his age (he was older than Colonel Ralston) made his presence a boon to the mess, especially during the early days, when the only recreation of an evening was "to put Daddy on the floor." Though he is no longer borne on the strength of the regiment, we feel sure he will always have a warm corner in his heart for the *taranwe nambar*[7] as the latter will always have for him.

There is no need to discuss the services of other officers of the Indian

---

[7] Hindi for 'ninth number.' (ed.)

Army Reserve. It will be sufficient to refer the reader to the table of casualties at the end of the book, where it will be seen that of the 12 officers who gave up their lives in the war, 4 belonged to the Indian Army Reserve, namely, Lieutenants Bright, Swaine, Wilsey, and Pearson, while the list of wounded includes the names of Lieutenants Wilsey, Walters, Oatway (twice), Scott, and Rigg.

The 1-1st Gurkhas also left the brigade at Damascus for India, though they did not embark until January, 1920.

The two regiments had fought beside each other for three years, in two campaigns, and in many actions.

There is no departure from the truth in saying that the 1-1st Gurkhas and 93rd can claim more battle honours, from the first Battle of Hannah, in January, 1916, to the Battle of Brown Hill, in September, 1918, than any other regiment of the 3rd Division.

On the repatriation of the 2-153rd Infantry in March, Captain Trevelyan rejoined the regiment, though his company (our old A Company) went with their new unit back to India, and Lieutenant Smith was demobilised, and returned to England.

Later in the year, dispatches were published. Lieutenant Colonel Ralston, who was only acting in the rank, received a brevet, while Captain Haycraft received a bar to his M.C., and Subadar Sheikh Abdullah the M.C.

Now that hostilities had ceased, sports became the most important event of the day. Our revival of hockey, after a lapse of five years, met with considerable success, and the regiment won the E.E.F. Hockey Championship at Cairo in April. In football, we were less fortunate, being beaten in the final by the 38th Central India Horse, after extra time, by 1-0.

Later, in the Damascus Week, we won, besides many running events, the Cross-Country Cup, and the Hockey and Football Tournaments, in both of the latter beating the 59th Rifles by 7-2, and 2-1, respectively.

Towards the end of the year, the complete evacuation of Syria by British troops took place, and in November the brigade moved by rail to Ludd, in Palestine, which was chosen as the permanent peace station of our brigade.

The old 9th Brigade that we had known, was now completely changed. The place of the 1-1st Gurkhas had been taken by the 21st Punjabis, while the Dorsets, who had been gradually demobilised down until there was nothing left, had been replaced, firstly by the Oxford and Bucks Light Infantry, and afterwards by a battalion of the West Riding Regiment.

Indian regiments were being slowly relieved by other units from India. The 105th Mahrattas departed in January 1920, and our turn came in April. With the departure of the 93rd, the last of the old 9th Brigade disappeared.

The regiment embarked on the *Kildonan Castle* on 26 April, and disembarked at Bombay on 8 May. Two days later the regiment detrained at Jubbulpore – curiously enough, the same station that it had left 5½ years before when it went on active service.

Appendix

British Officers
Killed

Captain	F. L. Dyer	Mesopotamia	[not recorded]
Captain	H. W. F. Ricketts	Gallipoli	[not recorded]
Lieutenant	R. J. K. Todd	Mesopotamia	21 January 1916
Lieutenant Colonel	S. R. Stevens	Mesopotamia	8 March 1916
Lieutenant	C. D. Bright	Mesopotamia	22 March 1916
Major	W. H. Simpson	Mesopotamia	17 April 1916
Captain	G. H. Barrett	Mesopotamia	24 April 1916
Captain	E. Cummings	Mesopotamia	27 April 1916
Lieutenant	J. G. Swaine	Mesopotamia	9 January 1917
Lieutenant Colonel	J. H. Whitehead*	Mesopotamia	11 January 1917
Lieutenant	E. H. Wilsey	Mesopotamia	11 January 1917
Lieutenant	Pearson	Mesopotamia	25 March 1917

Wounded

Captain	G. H. Barrett	Mesopotamia	21 January 1916
Captain	B. E. Morgan	Mesopotamia	8 March 1916
Major	H. L. Haughton	Mesopotamia	17 April 1916
Lieutenant	W. S. Haycraft	Mesopotamia	17 April 1916
Lieutenant	E. H. Wilsey	Mesopotamia	17 April 1916

Lieutenant	J. V. Drought	Mesopotamia	18 April 1916
Lieutenant	J. V. Drought	Mesopotamia	24 April 1916
Lieutenant	Walters	Mesopotamia	3 January 1917
Lieutenant Colonel	J. H. Whitehead	Mesopotamia	9 January 1917
Lieutenant	Challen	Mesopotamia	11 January 1917
Lieutenant Colonel	H. L Houghton	Mesopotamia	25 March 1917
Captain	A. C. Pegg	Mesopotamia	25 March 1917
Lieutenant	S. H. Oatway	Mesopotamia	25 March 1917
Lieutenant	J. V. Lalor	Mesopotamia	25 March 1917
Lieutenant	J. A. Scott	Mesopotamia	25 March 1917
Lieutenant	J. H. Rigg	Palestine	19 Sept 1918
Lieutenant	S. H. Oatway	Palestine	19 Sept 1918

* Died of wounds. The dates given are those on which the wounds were received

Indian Officers

Killed

Jemadar	Sayed Zaman	Mesopotamia	21 January 1916
Jemadar	Mul Singh	Mesopotamia	8 March 1916
Jemadar	Kadir Baksh	Mesopotamia	8 March 1916
Subadar	Gurmukh Singh	Mesopotamia	12 April 1916
Subadar Major	Muhammad Baksh*	Mesopotamia	14 April 1916
Subadar	Fazal Dad	Mesopotamia	11 January 1917
Subadar Major	Madat Khan	Mesopotamia	25 March 1917
Subadar	Wariam Singh	Mesopotamia	25 March 1917
Jemadar	Maghar Singh	Mesopotamia	25 March 1917

Wounded

Subadar Major	Muhammad Baksh	Mesopotamia	21 January 1916
Subadar	Narain Singh	Mesopotamia	8 March 1916
Jemadar	Mahbub Alam	Mesopotamia	8 March 1916
Jemadar	Majhi Khan	Mesopotamia	8 March 1916
Jemadar	Indar Singh	Mesopotamia	8 March 1916
Jemadar	Sher Khan	Mesopotamia	16 April 1916
Subadar	Partab Singh	Mesopotamia	17 April 1916
Subadar	Haram Singh	Mesopotamia	24 April 1916
Jemadar	Muhammad Din	Mesopotamia	24 April 1916
Jemadar	Taihal Singh	Mesopotamia	24 April 1916
Jemadar	Ghazan Khan	Mesopotamia	24 April 1916
Subadar	Indar Singh	Mesopotamia	15 July 1916
Jemadar	Saiyed Ahmed	Mesopotamia	18 October 1916

Jemadar	Sher Khan	Mesopotamia	9 January 1917
Jemadar	Hamam Singh	Mesopotamia	11 January 1917
Subadar	Bulaka Singh	Mesopotamia	25 March 1917
Subadar	Basant Singh	Mesopotamia	25 March 1917
Jemadar	Muhammad Sayed	Mesopotamia	25 March 1917

	Killed	Wounded	**Total**
British Officers	12	17	**29**
Indian Officers	9	18	**27**

* Died of wounds. The dates given are those on which the wounds were received

Table of Other Ranks Killed, Died Of Wounds, And Missing

2908	Sepoy	Allah Ditta	28 September 1915
3045	Sepoy	Kapur Singh	8 October 1915
3000	Sepoy	Pulla Khan,	18 October 1915
3039	Sepoy	Kala Khan,	28 October 1915
3012	Sepoy	Hayat Muhammad	4 November 1915
2841	Sepoy	Fazal Ilahi,	5 November 1915
2858	Naik	Fazal Khan*	14 November 1915
2299	Sepoy	Ghulam Kadir	21 January 1916
2623	Lance Naik	Lachhman Singh	21 January 1916
2721	Sepoy	Uttam Singh	21 January 1916
2791	Sepoy	Atma Singh	21 January 1916
3221	Sepoy	Partab Singh	21 January 1916
2743	Sepoy	Muhammad Shafi	21 January 1916
2944	Sepoy	Saudagar Singh	24 January 1916
2746	Lance Naik	Jagat Singh	26 January 1916
3257	Sepoy	Sher Ahmed	26 January 1916
2057	Sepoy	Uttam Singh	2 February 1916
3237	Sepoy	Shah Wali*	4 February 1916
2111	Naik	Abbas Khan	24 February 1916
2072	Naik	Mirza Khan	3 March 1916
1953	Havildar	Mahtab Singh	8 March 1916
2123	Havildar	Khuda Dad	8 March 1916
1613	Havildar	Rel Singh	8 March 1916
2962	Naik	Kala Khan	8 March 1916
2721	Lance Naik	Mehdi Khan	8 March 1916
2982	Lance Naik	Nawab Khan	8 March 1916
3058	Lance Naik	Imam Din	8 March 1916
3120	Lance Naik	Sher Ali	8 March 1916
2551	Lance Naik	Sawan Singh	8 March 1916
2749	Lance Naik	Kishan Singh	8 March 1916
3178	Sepoy	Hamam Singh	8 March 1916

3317	Sepoy	Buta Singh	8 March 1916
3037	Sepoy	Gurdial Singh	8 March 1916
3220	Sepoy	Fauja Singh	8 March 1916
2790	Sepoy	Sohan Singh	8 March 1916
3141	Sepoy	Ranga Singh	8 March 1916
3166	Sepoy	Gurbaksh Singh	8 March 1916
3135	Sepoy	Sadhu Singh	8 March 1916
3265	Sepoy	Udham Singh	8 March 1916
2910	Sepoy	Kabul Singh	8 March 1916
3280	Sepoy	Wali Khan,	8 March 1916
3095	Sepoy	Muhammad Afsar	8 March 1916
2922	Lance Naik	Ahmed Khan	8 March 1916
2882	Lance Naik	Allah Rakha	8 March 1916
3171	Lance Naik	Lal Khan	8 March 1916
3225	Sepoy	Tulsa Singh	8 March 1916
2422	Lance Naik	Basawa Singh	8 March 1916
1973	Sepoy	Chanan Singh+	8 March 1916
3472	Sepoy	Sapuran Singh+	8 March 1916
3332	Sepoy	Ganga Singh+	8 March 1916
2993	Sepoy	Makand Singh+	8 March 1916
3056	Sepoy	Allah Ditta*	9 March 1916
2864	Sepoy	Santa Singh*	10 March 1916
2930	Sepoy	Alif Din*	10 March 1916
3143	Sepoy	Mangat Singh*	11 March 1916
3025	Sepoy	Harnam Singh*	13 March 1916
3145	Sepoy	Shakar Khan*	14 March 1916
2911	Sepoy	Harnam Singh*	15 March 1916
1955	Sepoy	Sapuran Singh*	21 March 1916
3034	Sepoy	Faqir Muhammad	15 April 1916
3217	Sepoy	Jaimal Singh	16 April 1916
3070	Sepoy	Labh Singh	16 April 1916
2337	Naik	Diwan Singh	17 April 1916
2591	Naik	Tek Singh	17 April 1916
1741	Sepoy	Beunt Singh	17 April 1916

2528	Sepoy	Bahadur Singh	17 April 1916
3189	Sepoy	Teja Singh	17 April 1916
3003	Sepoy	Firoz Khan	17 April 1916
1714	Sepoy	Nek Muhammad	17 April 1916
2861	Sepoy	Muhammad Alam	17 April 1916
2650	Havildar	Hassain Shah+	17 April 1916
2288	Naik	Qasim Ali+	17 April 1916
3148	Sepoy	Kesar Singh+	17 April 1916
3191	Sepoy	Asa Singh+	17 April 1916
2348	Naik	Bagh Singh+	17 April 1916
2763	Sepoy	Sarain Singh*	18 April 1916
3493	Lance Naik	Bishan Singh*	20 April 1916
2850	Sepoy	Mahib Singh*	20 April 1916
3051	Sepoy	Naurang Singh*	23 April 1916
2954	Sepoy	Nawab Khan	24 April 1916
3080	Sepoy	Abdullah+	27 April 1916
3174	Sepoy	Bhagwan Singh*	8 May 1916
2917	Sepoy	Sher Zaman+	16 June 1916
3142	Sepoy	Dulip Singh	15 July 1916
252	Naik	Wali Muhammad	6 October 1916
3537	Sepoy	Kala	23 December 1916
2929	Havildar	Jiwan Khan	3 January 1917
3827	Sepoy	Ghulam Hussain	3 January 1917
3196	Sepoy	Lal Khan	3 January 1917
3420	Sepoy	Fazal Dad	3 January 1917
3249	Sepoy	Bostan Khan*	6 January 1917
1957	Havildar	Sarain Singh	9 January 1917
2612	Naik	Indar Singh	9 January 1917
3729	Sepoy	Kishan Singh	9 January 1917
3069	Sepoy	Lakha Singh	9 January 1919[8]

---

[8] The original source *does* give the date of 1919 but this is almost certainly an error for 1917 (ed.).

3224	Sepoy	Raja Khan	9 January 1917
1522	Sepoy	Dewa Singh	9 January 1917
1317	Sepoy	Mali Khan	9 January 1917
908	Sepoy	Dassunda Khan	10 January 1917
2558	Sepoy	Bhagat Singh*	10 January 1917
2271	Havildar	Ram Singh	11 January 1917
1452	Havildar	Wadhawa Singh	11 January 1917
2350	Havildar	Sohan Singh	11 January 1917
3683	Sepoy	Godar Khan	11 January 1917
3708	Sepoy	Ghulam Muhammad	11 January 1917
2481	Havildar	Hussain Baksh	11 January 1917
3737	Sepoy	Nur Zaman	11 January 1917
3149	Sepoy	Khan Muhammad	11 January 1917
3732	Sepoy	Mir Zamen	11 January 1917
3865	Sepoy	Lal Din	11 January 1917
3658	Sepoy	Muhammad Khan	11 January 1917
3367	Sepoy	Lachhman Singh	11 January 1917
3476	Sepoy	Puran Singh	11 January 1917
3744	Sepoy	Bakah Khan	11 January 1917
3752	Sepoy	Allah Dad	11 January 1917
3351	Sepoy	Rajwali*	12 January 1917
2875	Sepoy	Jagat Singh*	25 January 1917
4221	Sepoy	Kartar Singh	8 March 1917
2317	Havildar	Basant Singh	25 March 1917
2477	Naik	Bishan Singh	25 March 1917
2306	Sepoy	Bishan Singh	25 March 1917
2476	Sepoy	Mal Singh	25 March 1917
3024	Sepoy	Budh Singh	25 March 1917
3932	Sepoy	Chetu Singh	25 March 1917
2949	Sepoy	Bhan Singh	25 March 1917
2852	Sepoy	Kishan Singh	25 March 1917
3916	Sepoy	Matwali Khan	25 March 1917
3559	Sepoy	Faqir Khan	25 March 1917
3889	Sepoy	Gulab Khan	25 March 1917
3919	Sepoy	Mir Haider Shah	25 March 1917
2105	Havildar	Mehedi Khan+	25 March 1917

2304	Havildar	Harnam Singh+	25 March 1917
2446	Naik	Alias Khan+	25 March 1917
3055	Naik	Shera Khan+	25 March 1917
2717	Lance Naik	Ujager Singh+	25 March 1917
2445	Sepoy	Mhad Yar+	25 March 1917
3558	Sepoy	Din Muhammad+	25 March 1917
3689	Sepoy	Nur Alam+	25 March 1917
3835	Sepoy	Kharak Singh+	25 March 1917
3910	Sepoy	Nizam Din+	25 March 1917
3936	Sepoy	Ahmed Din+	25 March 1917
3942	Sepoy	Kala Khan+	25 March 1917
3986	Sepoy	Ruldu Khan+	25 March 1917
4016	Sepoy	Imam Din+	25 March 1917
3811	Sepoy	Bakar Din+	25 March 1917
435	Sepoy	Allah Dad+	25 March 1917
1119	SepoY	Nand Singh+	25 March 1917
3388	Sepoy	Harnam Singh+	25 March 1917
5427	Sepoy	Narain Singh+	25 March 1917
1181	Sepoy	Faiz Ali+	25 March 1917
3185	Sepoy	Ganga Singh*	26 March 1917
3789	Sepoy	Ghulam Haider*	2 April 1917
3643	Lance Naik	Sultan Khan*	28 May 1917
2834	Sepoy	Shahwali*[9]	25 June 1917
4919	Sepoy	Baghel Singh	13 July 1917
3991	Sepoy	Muhammad Roshan+	13 July 1917
3444	Sepoy	Bhan Singh*	13 July 1917
3404	Sepoy	Talok Singh*	19 July 1917
4284	Sepoy	Shah Dad*	22 August 1917
3410	Sepoy	Mangal Singh*	8 June 1918
2842	Havildar	Saif Ali	19 Sept 1918
1769	Sepoy	Arjan Singh	19 Sept 1918
3768	Sepoy	Hayat Muhammad	19 Sept1918
3395	Sepoy	Muhammad Amir	19 Sept 1918

---

[9] Although recorded as Shahwali it is probable that the man's name was actually Shah Wali. (ed.)

3527	Sepoy	Khan Zaman	19 Sept 1918
3609	Sepoy	Muhammad Khan	19 Sept 1918
4311	Sepoy	Pir Baksh	19 Sept 1918
4014	Sepoy	Muhammad Khan	19 Sept 1918
4271	Sepoy	Ram Singh	19 Sept 1918
4963	Sepoy	Tara Singh*	22 Sept 1918
4480	Sepoy	Haidar Khan*	27 Sept 1918

* Died of wounds
+ Missing

Total Officers Killed or died of wounds	21
Total other ranks killed, died of wounds and missing	173[10]
Total Other ranks died of disease	41[11]
Total	**235**

---

[10] This total is in the original but the list contains only 171 names. (ed.)
[11] No names are given for this total. (ed.)

www.ingramcontent.com/pod-product-compliance
Lightning Source LLC
Chambersburg PA
CBHW071205070526
44584CB00019B/2925